EXPERIMENTAL DESIGN AND ANALYSIS

A Systematic Approach

Richard P. Honeck
Clare T. Kibler
Judith Sugar

UNIVERSITY
PRESS OF
AMERICA

LANHAM • NEW YORK • LONDON

Copyright © 1983 by

University Press of America,™ Inc.

4720 Boston Way
Lanham, MD 20706

3 Henrietta Street
London WC2E 8LU England

Printed in the United States of America

ISBN (Perfect): 0-8191-3104-0

TO

Joan and Jon

and

M, D, A, G, M, M, and R

CONTENTS

PREFACE

Over the years a number of graduate students at the University of Cincinnati have learned the system presented in this book and have provided comments. Their comments have helped to clarify various ideas presented in the book. Tony Frankfurter, Dave Micco, Paul Riechmann, Mary Stefl, Kathy Voegtle and especially Shig Kuwada, deserve mention in this regard. Years ago, Shig enthusiastically argued that "the system" ought to be published and helped write early drafts of some of the chapters in this book. Bringing the book to camera-ready condition was a grueling, demanding task, but Garnett Pugh and Diane Frank put the manuscript on word processing equipment and made our task easier. We particularly appreciate Diane's efforts in computerizing the entire manuscript, down to the last aggravating subscript. Karen Wall also deserves our gratitude for having typed several drafts of most of the chapters. Finally, we are grateful to the Literary Executor of the late Sir Ronald A. Fisher, F.R.S., to Dr. Frank Yates, F.R.S., and to Longman Group Ltd., London, for permission to reprint Table V, in rearranged form, from their book, Statistical Tables for Biological, Agricultural and Medical Research (6th Edition, 1974). This book was written with the firm conviction that some fundamentals of experimental design and analysis can be taught more adequately than hitherto has been the case. We hope that the book realizes this goal and that the reader learns as much in reading it as we did in writing it.

INTRODUCTION

All experiments in the behavioral sciences use subjects (i.e., organisms) that are exposed to treatments of one kind or another. Rarely, however, do experimenters use just two treatments, such as an experimental and control group. More often, they use several treatments. In fact, a large vocabulary has developed for identifying these multi-treatment designs including completely randomized designs, factorial designs, treatments-by-subjects designs, and so on. Unfortunately, texts on experimental design frequently bandy these names about without explaining the basics of experimental design. Moreover, the names are not used in any taxonomically meaningful way; they tend to be idiosyncratic so that they do not reflect properties common to all designs. The problem of relating one design to another arises from the vast number of ways in which subject, treatment, and other experimental factors can relate to one another. Fortunately, there is a system to these relationships. This text attempts to explain this system, and to clear the ground for a coherent taxonomy of experimental designs.

As experimental designs have become more complex, statistical analysis of the data connected with these designs has become correspondingly complex. The statistical procedure most often used in conjunction with multi-treatment experimental designs is analysis of variance. A fact of experimental life is that scores differ from one another -- in other words, they vary. The analysis of variance is a technique for dividing up this variability into "pieces" and then comparing measures of variability to one another in order to decide whether some particular piece of variability is due to chance. That is all it tells us, but it is complex nonetheless.

Thus the modern experimenter is often faced with two interrelated tasks -- constructing an appropriate

1

multi-treatment design and selecting a proper analysis of variance for the data generated by the design. The first task is much more difficult, primarily because it requires knowledge of the content area of the experiment as well as an understanding of design construction. Expertise in design construction entails knowing how to relate subject, treatment, and other experimental factors to get a clear picture of the effect of treatments. In any event, once a design has been constructed, it strongly suggests a particular way of analyzing the variance in the data. The primary goal of the present text is to show how experimental designs and the analysis of variance are interconnected.

THE GENERAL NOTATION SYSTEM (GNS)

Experimental designs are constructed by observing some systematic rules. These rules are primarily concerned with the relationship between subjects and the experimental treatments they receive. This text attempts to explain what these rules are, how the designs that result from their application can be symbolized, and how the symbolization can be used in conjunction with the analysis of variance. The result of this effort, and the focus of this text, is a General Notation System (GNS) that can be used in connection with most of the experimental designs currently being used.

There are two aspects to the GNS. The first is an integrated, comprehensive approach to the taxonomy problem -- i.e., how to name designs. Because the design names follow directly from the relationships among the subject, treatment, and other experimental factors, an investigator who understands the naming system is in a better position to construct appropriate designs. The GNS is not a cookbook approach -- it requires genuine understanding of the basics of experimental design rather than rote memorization of particular kinds of designs. For this reason, it discourages the strategy of saying, "Well, here's the kind of design I think I have. Now let's see if I can find it in a book," or worse yet, of saying, "Here's a design in the book, maybe I can fit this to my needs."

The advantages of the GNS go well beyond those that accrue from an efficient notation system. The GNS also allows the investigator to quickly and accurately carry out certain conceptual and mathematical analysis of variance procedures. The GNS describes simple rules for quickly and accurately obtaining pieces of information needed for any analysis of variance -- sources of variance, degrees of freedom, expected mean squares, and error terms. That is, using the GNS makes it simple to obtain a desired component of the analysis of variance. These components can be obtained before data is collected. Certain components (e.g., mean squares, F ratios) to which the GNS does not apply are obtained afterwards, since they are mathematical in nature and depend on the actual data.

RELATIONSHIP TO OTHER DESIGN TEXTS

The present text differs from traditional texts on experimental design in two basic ways. First, it covers far fewer topics than are covered in these texts because we have chosen to present only the GNS. This keeps the book focused and short! Material which is not covered can be found in standard texts on experimental design such as those by Edwards (1972), Keppel (1973), Kirk (1968), Lee (1975), Myers (1979), and Winer (1962).

Obviously the present text covers some of the same topics as the texts just referred to. However, and this is the second difference, these topics are not covered in the same way. In contrast to traditional design texts, we use the GNS to emphasize basic similarities in all designs. Our treatment of analysis of variance topics is also different. Traditional texts discuss each of these topics (e.g., sources of variance) every time a new type of design is introduced so that coverage of each topic is spread out across several chapters. We believe that this strategy generally fails to get across the point that there are rules for obtaining pieces of information relevant to any analysis of variance. In other words, the rules of the game don't change when you leave town. The present text attempts to make this clear. Just as importantly, the text emphasizes a verbal rather than mathematical explanation of analysis of variance concepts. Most consumers of experimental design texts are not mathematically sophisticated. Hence, a jungle of mathematical expressions and formulas may only serve to frustrate the otherwise intelligent reader who could profit immensely from verbal discussions. Finally, because the text's coverage of analysis of variance topics flows from a general notation system that simplifies experimental design structure, the connections between the topics and designs become clearer. Moreover, the GNS highlights the intimate relationship between analysis of variance topics.

Other authors such as Keppel (1973), Lee (1975), Millman and Glass (1967), and Myers (1979) use notations for experimental designs that are similar to our notation. However, their notations are not presented as bonafide systems for constructing designs. Hence, these notation systems seem to lack generality. These authors also offer rules for obtaining the necessary pieces of information associated with an analysis of variance. However, we generally do not find their rules to be streamlined or memorable. The reason, we believe, is that the rules do not have the advantage of flowing from a systematic treatment of the basics in design construction. These comments are not meant as criticisms since the systems were not written to accomplish these goals. In contrast, however, they were the primary goals in writing this text.

COMPUTER APPLICATIONS

Several computer programs are available that carry out analysis of variance procedures. These include the Biomedical (BMDP) package (Dixon, 1981), the Statistical Analysis System (SAS) package (Helwig & Council, 1979), and the Statistical Package for the Social Sciences (SPSS) edited by Nie et al (1975). The SPSS procedures are, as of November, 1982, less versatile than either the BMDP or SAS procedures.

That is, SPSS handles a limited variety of experimental designs. For example, it cannot handle either repeated measures or hierarchical designs, both of which will be discussed in this book in relation to the General Notation System. The 1979 update of SPSS (Hull & Nie, 1979) does not appear to remedy these deficiencies. In contrast, both the BMDP and SAS procedures are capable of handling a wide variety of experimental designs including all those that fall within the purview of the General Notation System. Moreover, both of these packages use notation systems that are similar to the General Notation System. Thus, familiarity with the GNS will facilitate immensely the understanding of these packages.

ORGANIZATION OF THE TEXT

There are three major divisions in the text. Chapter 1 explains the basics of design construction and the GNS. It is the heart of the text and must be mastered before proceeding. Read the chapter or parts of it as often as necessary. Then complete the exercises at the end of the chapter. Chapter 2 presents the basic concepts and logic behind the analysis of variance. It also should be read as often as necessary since it provides background for understanding the remaining chapters. Chapters 3 through 6 expand on particular concepts discussed in Chapter 2 and show how they are used in conjunction with experimental designs. Each chapter uses the GNS to relate a particular analysis of variance concept to experimental designs. Once again, complete the exercises at the end of each chapter since you will gain some experience working with the designs and get some feedback on your understanding of design concepts.

We hope that you enjoy the text while learning from it. Once the GNS is mastered, you will have available a facile system for constructing, selecting, and analyzing experimental designs. If you wish to comment on the book, for good or bad, write to Richard P. Honeck, Department of Psychology, University of Cincinnati, Cincinnati, Ohio 45221.

EXPERIMENTAL DESIGN

AND THE

GENERAL NOTATION SYSTEM (GNS)

The reader must master this chapter. It is pre-requisite to an understanding of the system presented in the following chapters. Read the chapter, or sections of it, as many times as necessary and complete the exercises before proceeding. The reasons for emphasizing this chapter are simple. It is the authors' belief that few if any texts on design provide a solid grounding in the basics. Rather, they quickly launch into a discussion of different types of design without explaining the typology used and, unfortunately, without discussing the commonalities among all designs. The present chapter attempts to familiarize the reader with the basic building blocks of design and with the General Notation System which capitalizes on this knowledge. A good command of design allows the investigator to make a wise choice between alternative designs, to have more than a mechanical understanding of the statistics used in conjunction with a design, and to clearly communicate the nature of the design. Furthermore, the ability to evaluate experiments improves.

LAYOUT OF AN EXPERIMENTAL DESIGN

The layout of an experiment is a schematic or diagrammatic representation of the relationship between experimental factors. At a glance, the diagram yields detailed knowledge of a design. This chapter provides the basics for constructing and interpreting layouts. There is nothing tricky or complex about them. Moreover, there is no standard way of diagramming, although some guidelines for constructing diagrams will be offered. Before proceeding, however, some basic concepts in experimental design need to be explained.

First, let's discuss the concept of experimental factor. Unfortunately, it is not an easy concept to define. Experimental factors come in an amazing variety of forms. Perhaps the only thing that distinguishes experimental factors from non-experimental factors is that experimental factors are intrinsic to the experiment. For example, in behavioral research, subjects are obviously intrinsic since studies could not be done without them. Moreover, the investigator is usually interested in the effect of certain treatments that subjects receive. Finally, a design may contain "nuisance" or pseudo factors which the investigator is not particularly interested in but whose presence is nevertheless beneficial and thus cannot be ignored in the analysis.

These three types of experimental factors, subject, treatment, and pseudo, are illustrated quite simply. Suppose we are interested in determining which of two drugs, drug X or drug Y, is most effective in alleviating the symptoms of some disease. We randomly select four hospitals from the set of hospitals in a city and also randomly select 10 patients with the disease from each of the hospitals. The 10 patients at each of two hospitals get drug X and 10 patients at each of the other two hospitals get drug Y. That is, 40 subjects get drugs, 20 receive drug X and 20 receive drug Y. The patients with the disease are obviously the subject factor. The treatment factor is drugs. The four hospitals constitute the pseudo factor, since our major interest is in the effect of the drugs, not in the effect of hospitals. However, we may have had to select four hospitals in order to get enough patients with the disease. Moreover, the use of different hospitals rather than a single hospital probably adds to the generalizability of the results; i.e., the extent to which the results would validly apply to all patients with the disease rather than just those at a certain hospital.

A number of non-experimental factors would enter into the drug study, some relating to the drug, such as dosage level, time and manner of administration, and so on, and some relating to the patient such as age, sex, physical health, etc. These factors would undoubtedly have to be controlled. Other non-experimental factors such as room lighting, size of bed, etc., might be allowed to vary freely if their influence on drug effectiveness was considered inconsequential. The point is simply that the investigator is interested in the relative effectiveness of drugs X and Y in alleviating the symptoms of a particular disease. He or she is not specifically interested in the most effective mode of administration, dosage level, sex differences, and so on, but since these factors could influence the results they must be controlled. Actually, any one of the non-experimental factors might become the focus of study in a different investigation and therefore assume the status of an experimental factor.

In general, we will divide the world of experimental factors into three parts -- subject factors, treatment factors, and pseudo factors. Subject and treatment factors are present in all experimental designs. A pseudo factor may or may not be present depending upon the practical and theoretical requirements of an experiment. Finally, note that an experimental factor varies quantitatively (in amount) or qualitatively (in kind). For example, subjects obviously differ from one another in many ways, such as intelligence and age, which are quantifiable, and in religion, political affiliation, etc., which might be considered qualitative. In the extreme case, if only one subject was used in an experiment, the subject factor would not vary. Variation between subjects is usually controlled by randomly assigning subjects to treatments. Similarly, treatment factors and pseudo factors may also vary quantitatively or qualitatively. In the drug example, two different kinds of drugs were used, so the drug factor varied in a qualitative way. The same is true for the hospital factor. In general, the variations within an experimental factor can be called levels regardless of whether the variation is quantitative or qualitative. In the drug experiment, the subject factor contains 40 levels, the pseudo factor contains 4 levels, and the treatment factor contains 2 levels. This book will use capital letters for experimental factors and small letters for the levels of these factors. In the drug study, the three experimental factors are S' (Subjects), H' (Hospitals), and D (Drugs). The levels of S' are s_1, s_2, s_3 ... s_{40}; the levels of H' are h_1, h_2, h_3, and h_4; and the levels of D are d_1 and d_2.

The preceding discussion leads to the following definitions of subject, treatment, and pseudo factors.

Subject factor: The organisms used in an experiment.

Treatment factor: A factor which is manipulated in order to determine its effect upon the dependent variable; also called an independent variable.

Pseudo factor: Any non-subject factor which is included in a design in order to increase the efficiency of the effect of the treatment factor; sometimes called a nuisance factor.

All three factors are experimental factors since they are intrinsic to the experiment itself. Obviously subject and treatment factors are intrinsic to any experiment in the behavioral sciences since the experiment could not be done without them. A pseudo factor may or may not be used, depending on the experimenter's purposes. However, if a pseudo factor is included, it usually allows a more accurate estimate of the effects of the treatment factor. In the drug example above, use of the pseudo factor allows the researcher to isolate variability in the data contributed by using various hospitals from that contributed by using various drugs. In notating a design, all and only experimental factors should be specified.

Finally, we should distinguish between <u>random factors</u> and <u>fixed factors</u>. A factor is random <u>if all the levels</u> of that factor have an equal opportunity of being chosen. Hays (1963) provides a more technical, mathematical definition of a random variable. From an operational standpoint, however, a factor can be considered random if no systematic bias is consciously exercised in the choice of the levels of that factor. Thus, if some factor has 100 discrete levels, and a sample of 10 levels is chosen by use of a table of random numbers, or by blindly selecting 10 marbles from a jar containing marbles numbered 1 to 100, or by a similar procedure, then the 10 levels that are chosen can be considered a random sample. Consequently, a factor with randomly chosen levels is termed random. In the drug study, the Subject and Hospital factors are random. A factor is fixed if the levels of that factor were deliberately and purposely chosen. The Drug factor is fixed since the experimenter purposely selected drug X and drug Y; that is, levels of the Drug factor were not randomly sampled from the population of all possible drugs. In this book, the subject factor will always be random. Pseudo and treatment factors may be either random or fixed, although pseudo factors are usually random and treatment factors are usually fixed. Finally, whether a factor is random or fixed determines the inferences one can make. Specifically, if a factor is random, one can generalize back to the population from which the levels of that factor were drawn, but if a factor is fixed one can only generalize back to the particular levels of the factors that were used in the experiment.

RELATIONSHIPS BETWEEN EXPERIMENTAL DESIGN FACTORS

There are two basic relationships between experimental factors -- crossing and nesting.

Crossing: Factors are <u>completely crossed</u> if all levels of a given factor occur at each level of the other factor. Factors are <u>partially crossed</u> if at least one, but not all, levels of one factor occur at all levels of another factor.

Suppose two subjects are run in an experiment with two levels of the treatment factor, A. If both subjects are exposed to both treatments, then S' and A are completely crossed, since all levels of one factor occur at each level of the other factor. If one subject (s_1) is exposed to a single treatment (a_1) while the other subject (s_2) is exposed to both treatments (a_1 and a_2), then S' and A are partially crossed, since only some levels of one factor (s_2 but not s_1) occur at more than one level of another factor.

Nesting: An experimental factor is <u>completely nested</u> in another factor if <u>each</u> level of one factor occurs at only one level of the other factor. Experimental factors are <u>partially nested</u>: (a) if each level of both factors occurs at some, but not all, levels of the other and (b) if at least one level of one factor occurs at least at two levels of the other.

Suppose factor A has four levels, a_1, a_2, a_3, and a_4, and factor B has two levels, b_1 and b_2. If a_1 and a_2 occur at b_1, forming the combinations b_1a_1 and b_1a_2 and a_3 and a_4 occur at b_2, forming the combinations b_2a_3 and b_2a_4, then factor A is said to be completely nested in factor B. The factor which includes the other is the <u>nesting factor</u> and the factor which is included is the <u>nested factor</u>. In this example, B is the nesting factor since each level of B includes unique levels of A, and A is the nested factor since each level of A occurs at only one level of B. In the case of partial nesting, both factors are nested and both factors do some nesting. For example, suppose factors A and B each have three levels (at least three of one factor and two of the other are needed to illustrate partial nesting -- try it!). If a_1 occurs at b_1 and b_2, a_2 occurs at b_3, and a_3 occurs at b_2, then factors A and B are partially nested. Clearly, no levels of the factors are crossed, yet at least one level of each factor occurs with two levels of the other.

11

The General Notation System is not applicable to designs that involve either partial crossing or partial nesting so such designs are not considered in this text. More advanced texts can be consulted for discussion of these designs. In any event, keep the following "red flag" in mind.

NOTE: The General Notation System does not handle designs that involve partial crossing or partial nesting.

Now we can compare crossing and nesting. Complete nesting exists between two factors if there is no overlap in the levels of one factor within levels of a second; that is, unique levels of one factor occur at each level of a second factor. In the preceding paragraph, if s_1 is run at a_1, and s_2 at a_2, then a nesting relationship exists between S' and A. Complete crossing exists any time there is total overlap between levels of two or more factors. Traditional terms for completely crossed are <u>factorial</u> and <u>orthogonal</u>. It should be clear that complete crossing produces a symmetrical relationship between factors in the sense that if factor A is crossed with factor B, then B is also crossed with A. By contrast, nesting relationships are asymmetrical since, for example, if A is nested in B, then B cannot be nested in A. Designs employing complete nesting or complete crossing can now be considered in detail.

Designs Involving Nesting

Suppose that one group of 10 college students memorizes a list of long sentences and a second group of 10 students memorizes a list of short sentences. Here, subjects are nested in Sentence Length, the treatment factor. In other words, the S' factor has 20 levels, where 10 of these occur at one level (l_1) of Length and the other 10 levels at the other level (l_2) of Length. Sentence Length is the nesting factor and College Students is the nested factor.

The design above can be symbolized as $S'_{10}(L_2)$, where S' stands for Subject and L stands for Length of sentence. This notation indicates several things:

(a) Ten subjects are nested in each of two levels of
L. In other words, 10 levels of the S' factor occur
at each of the two levels of the L factor. The
subscripts indicate the number of levels of one factor
that occur at levels of the other factors. If a
nesting relationship holds between factors, the
subscripts indicate how many levels of the nested
factor occur at each distinct level of the nesting
factor. (b) A nesting relationship is, in general,
indicated by parentheses or brackets. As previously
mentioned, a nesting relationship is asymmetrical;
that is, it goes in only one direction, left to right.
Parentheses around a symbol(s) [e.g., (L)] indicate
the nesting factor(s). The symbol immediately
preceding the parentheses is the nested factor. In
the $S'_{10}(L_2)$ design, the S' factor is nested in the L
factor since it is immediately left of the parentheses. The L factor is not nested in anything since
there is no factor to its immediate right which is
enclosed in parentheses. This design notation can be
read as, "Subjects nested in Length." In traditional
terminology, the S'(L) design is one kind of
completely randomized design. (c) The total number of
observations is 20 or 10 x 2. In the example, the
total number of observations equals the total number
of subjects since only one measure is taken on each
subject. Later on, we will consider designs in which
repeated measures are taken on each subject. (d) The
prime above the S indicates that Subjects is a random
factor, while the absence of the prime above L
indicates that Sentence Length is a fixed factor. (e)
There is no overlap in the symbols used to designate
the factors. There is an S and an L, but not two Ss
or two Ls. In general, it does not matter what
symbols are used to designate factors, but no symbol
should be used more than once since symbol repetition
would obviously be confusing. However, it is
convenient to always symbolize the Subject factor as
S'. A diagram of this design is presented in Table
1.1.

Table 1.1

An $S'_{10}(L_2)$ Design

_____

l_1 $\quad$ $\begin{array}{c} s_1 \\ \cdot \\ \cdot \\ \cdot \\ s_{10} \end{array}$

l_2 $\quad$ $\begin{array}{c} s_{11} \\ \cdot \\ \cdot \\ \cdot \\ s_{20} \end{array}$

_____

A final point about the $S'_{10}(L_2)$ design is worth detailed discussion. There is only one nest in this design, i.e., only one factor is nested. However, other so-called <u>Hierarchical</u> designs may involve double, triple, and possibly higher degrees of nesting, the limit being imposed by practical and theoretical considerations. Hierarchical designs involving three or more degrees of nesting are extremely rare but possible. The drug study mentioned earlier was an example of a Hierarchical design -- 10 patients at each of two hospitals received drug X and 10 patients at each of two different hospitals received drug Y. Patients is the Subject factor, Hospitals the pseudo factor, and Drugs the treatment factor. The Subject factor is nested in the Hospital factor which, in turn, is nested in the Drug factor. This design is symbolized $S'_{10}[H'_2(D_2)]$. Note the brackets and parentheses. The combination of brackets and parentheses is being used for visual convenience only. Two sets of parentheses or two sets of brackets could be used just as well. The parentheses indicate that H' is nested in D, and the brackets indicate that S' is nested in H'(D). This suggests that the Drug factor is the <u>ultimate nesting factor</u> since the other two factors are nested in it, but it is not nested in any other factor. Thus, S' is nested in H', but because H' is itself nested in D, S' is ultimately nested in D. (In this text, only designs involving an equal number of levels of the nested factor at each level of the nesting factor will be considered.)

14

Notice the following additional characteristics of the $S'_{10}[H'_2(D_2)]$ design. First, it can be read, "S' nested within H' and H' nested in D," or, more briefly, "S' within H' within D." The pseudo factor is H', as mentioned previously. In general, a pseudo factor is any non-subject factor which is nested. The "pseudoness" of the H' factor would show up in an analysis of variance of the data. This analysis would yield only three sources of variance -- D, H'(D), and S'(H'(D)). So H' cannot be isolated as a source of variance. Any investigator who ran this design with the intention of examining effects due to H' would be quite disappointed. The moral should be clear: an investigator must know how the experimental factors are related because this relationship determines what factors and factor combinations can be isolated as sources of variance. Finally, the $S'_{10}[H'_2(D_2)]$ notation indicates that S' and H' are random but D is fixed, and that there is a total of 40 or 10 x 2 x 2 observations, one observation per subject. This design is diagrammed in Table 1.2.

Designs Involving Crossing

The second basic type of relationship between experimental factors is crossing, which has already been defined. We will consider only completely crossed designs which are also balanced, that is, in which all the combinations occur equally often (Hays, 1963). Unbalanced designs are rare, so we will not concern ourselves with them. Moreover, only those designs involving an equal number (n) of observations in each experimental cell (treatment level or treatment combination) will be considered. Experiments with unequal n, and the problems they pose, are discussed in most traditional design texts (e.g., Myers, 1979).

Perhaps the simplest case of complete crossing of factors involves repeated measurements on the same subjects. Suppose that 10 subjects are asked to solve three different kinds of problems, and the time taken to solve each problem is measured. The subjects receive the problems in random order. Because each subject's performance is measured more than once, the design involves a repeated measure. The S' factor and the Problem (P) factor are crossed since each level of

Table 1.2

An $S'_{10}[H'_2(D_2)]$ Design

		s_1
	h_1	$\cdot$
		$\cdot$
		$\cdot$
		s_{10}
d_1		
		s_{11}
	h_2	$\cdot$
		$\cdot$
		$\cdot$
		s_{20}
		s_{21}
	h_3	$\cdot$
		$\cdot$
		$\cdot$
		s_{30}
d_2		
		s_{31}
	h_4	$\cdot$
		$\cdot$
		$\cdot$
		s_{40}

the S' factor occurs at each level of the P factor and vice versa. This design is symbolized $S'_{10}P_3$, indicating that each of 10 subjects is measured at each of the three P levels. Therefore, 30 observations are made. Note that S' is a random factor, as indicated by the prime ('), and that P is a fixed factor since the experimenter is interested in performance on three specific problem types. Note also that since there is no nesting in the design, there are no parentheses in the notation. Table 1.3 shows one way of diagramming this design.

Table 1.3

An $S'_{10}P_3$ Design

```
----------------------------------
            P_1      P_2      P_3
      s
       1
       .
       .       -------------------->
       .
      s
       10
----------------------------------
```

Simple crossed designs such as S'P can be expanded by adding new levels of P (i.e., additional
problems) to obtain $S'P_4$, $S'P_5$, etc., or by crossing
new factors with the original S' and P factors.
Experimenters often cross factors to determine whether
they interact. An <u>interaction</u> is present if the
effect of the levels of one factor depends on the
levels of the other factor(s). Suppose we are interested in a possible interaction between Problem type
and environmental Distraction, for instance, music vs.
speech. The Distraction (D) factor is easily added to
the $S'_{10}P_3$ design by crossing it with S' and P to yield
an $S'_{10}P_3D_2$ design. In the latter design there are 6
or 3 x 2 treatment combinations and each subject
receives all six, usually in random order, for a total
of 60 observations. Specifically, every subject would
solve each problem type twice, once in the presence of
music, and once in the presence of speech. The S'PD
notation is read as, "S' repeated across a factorial
combination of P and D," or simply as, "S' across P
across D," or just, "S' across PD." Look at Table 1.4
for a diagram of this design. Clearly, new factors
could be crossed ad infinitum with existing factors,
the limits of the crossing being determined by
interests, hypotheses to be tested, etc.

Table 1.4

An $S'_{10}P_3D_2$ Design

	d_1				d_2		
	p_1	p_2	p_3		p_1	p_2	p_3
s_1							
.							
.		-------------------------------------->					
.							
s_{10}							

Designs Involving Both Nesting and Crossing

Many designs involve some combination of nesting and crossing. The possibilities are numerous. First, consider an S'(A)B design, where A and B are general designations for experimental factors. This design can be read, "S' nested in A across B," since subjects are nested in A and crossed with B, the repeated measure. Factors A and B are completely crossed, i.e., all possible combinations of A and B levels occur. Insofar as the relationship between A and B is concerned, the enclosure of A within parentheses is irrelevant because the notation is read from left to right. Therefore, (A)B specifies the same relationship between A and B as does AB. The parentheses around A indicate only that subjects are nested in the levels of A.

Suppose each of 10 college students is given the same unsolvable problem. After some time limit on the problem, five subjects are told that they are doing well, working above average, etc., and the other five are told that they are doing poorly, working below average, etc. After this feedback, each subject is asked to rate how well he or she expects to do on subsequent trials. The same type of feedback is given 10 times and, after each feedback, a rating measure is obtained. Thus there are two groups, and every

18

subject in both groups is measured 10 times. The notation for this design is $S_5'(F_2)T_{10}$ where F stands for Feedback and T for Trials. Table 1.5 is a diagram of this design.

Table 1.5

An $S_5'(F_2)T_{10}$ Design

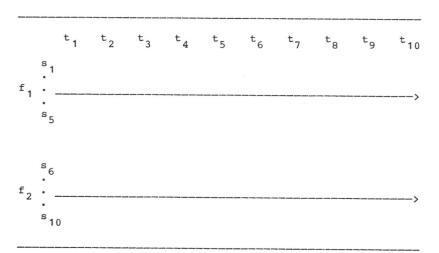

Notice that there may be more than one repeated measure in a design. In the feedback example suppose that three different problems (P) are given, one per experimental session. Then the design becomes $S_5'(F_2)T_{10}P_3$, and both T and P are repeated measures. This design can be read, "S' nested within F and repeated across a factorial combination of T and P," or more simply as, "S' within F across TP." Note that F, T, and P are crossed.

In contrast to the S'(A)B design, consider an S'A(B) design. The enclosure of B within parentheses indicates that A, but not S', is nested in B. The resulting combinations constitute the repeated measure, that is, subjects are repeated across the A(B) combinations. Suppose an experimenter is interested in the effect of pictures on a child's reading ability. After controlling for factors such as vocabulary, four children's books are selected at random and two of them are reprinted without the usual

19

illustrations. Twenty children from a local school are then taught to read from these books. The order of books is randomized across the subjects, each of whom reads all four books. After each book is completed, a standardized reading test is administered. A possible notation for this design is $S'_{20}B'_2(P_2)$ where B' stands for books and P stands for pictures. Note that the B' factor is nested in the P factor since each level of B' occurs at only one level of P. Note also that these combinations are repeated across subjects, and that the B' factor is random, since the experimenter is interested in all children's books, with or without illustrations.

Next, consider an S'(AB) design. Here, subjects are nested in a factorial (crossed) combination of A and B. The notation can be read, "S' nested within AB." In other words, a given subject receives a treatment that represents one of the combinations of A and B. No repeated measures are taken. (At least, this is a strict interpretation of this notation. The problem is that experimenters often take repeated measures on each subject and combine these measures into a single value.) Suppose an S'(AB) design in which one group of five males and one group of five females are exposed to a low level of frustration, and similarly, two different groups are exposed to a high level of frustration. Degree of aggression is the dependent variable. This design can be symbolized $S'_5(X_2F_2)$ where X stands for Sex and F for Frustration. Among other things, this notation indicates that there are four treatment combinations, i.e., five subjects "receive" x_1f_1, five "receive" x_1f_2, five "receive" x_2f_1, and five "receive" x_2f_2. If the subjects in this experiment were measured over a series of trials (T), say 10, then the design would be symbolized $S'_5(X_2F_2)T_{10}$, indicating that S' is nested in a factorial (crossed) combination of X and F, and crossed with T, the repeated measure. The $S'_5(X_2F_2)T_{10}$ design is illustrated in Table 1.6.

Table 1.6

An $S_5'(X_2F_2)T_{10}$ Design

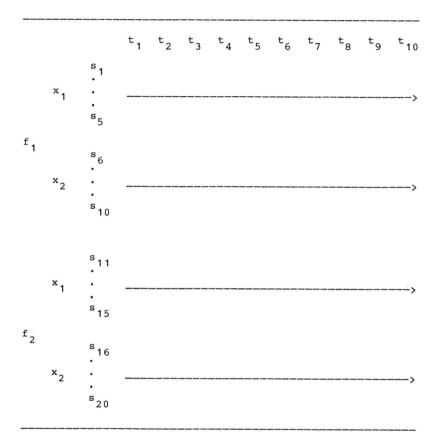

The reader should now be able to understand designs that many find mind boggling. Consider, for example, an S'[A'(B)]C design. The notation can be read as, "S' nested within A' nested within B across C" or as "S' within A' within B across C." In other words, S' is nested in A', A' and S' are nested in B, since B is the ultimate nesting factor, and S', A', and B are crossed with C.

This design is illustrated quite easily. Suppose we are interested in comparing the effectiveness of three different methods of teaching mathematics. We randomly select six elementary schools from a city. Each teaching method is used at two schools, that is, method X at schools 1 and 2, method Y at schools 3 and 4, and method Z at schools 5 and 6. Each method is used for some specified time period on each of five days, with each child's progress measured each day. This design can be symbolized $S'_n[C'_2(M_3)]D_5$, where C' represents School, M represents teaching Method, and D represents Day. The notation indicates that some unspecified number (n) of subjects is nested in the School factor, School is nested in Method, and each subject is measured five times. This is a Hierarchical design with one repeated measure. It is hierarchical because more than one nesting relationship is present. Note that D, the repeated measure, is crossed with all other factors. One consequence of this is that any interaction between Methods and Days can be evaluated. This design is diagrammed in Table 1.7.

In sum, experimental designs involve two basic types of relationships between experimental factors, nesting and/or crossing. A given design may involve nesting, e.g., $S'(A)$, $S'[A(B)]$, etc., or crossing, e.g., $S'A$, $S'AB$, etc., or both nesting and crossing, e.g., $S'(A)B$, $S'(A)B'C$, $S'(AB)C$, $S'(A(B))C$, etc. The reader should now have the knowledge to generate his or her own illustrations, verbal or diagrammatic, for any notation or, conversely, to translate illustrations and descriptions into the notation system.

Table 1.7

An $S_n'[C_2'(M_3)]D_5$ Design

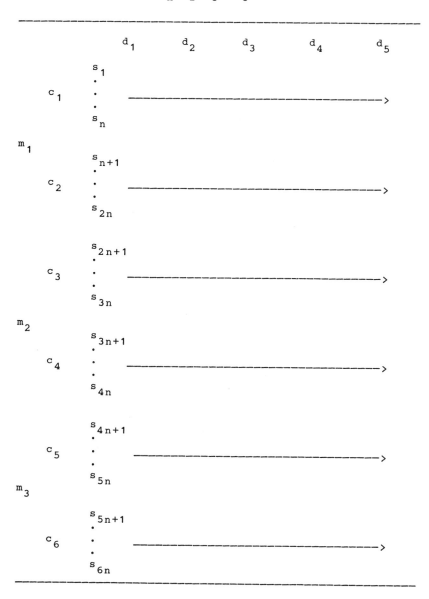

BASIC TYPES OF DESIGN

The notation system makes it convenient to discuss three basic design types -- Between Subjects, Within Subjects, and Mixed. These types are defined in terms of the relationship(s) between the subject factor and the other experimental factors. The relationships among the other experimental factors are irrelevant to the design type.

In a Between design the subjects are nested, and in a pure Between design only one measure is taken on each subject. Examples of Between designs are S'(A), S'(AB), S'(A'(B)), etc. In these designs a particular subject is exposed to only one treatment or treatment combination. Thus, these designs are also called Between Subjects designs.

A Within design involves a crossed relationship between the subject factor and other factors. In a pure Within design each subject experiences all the conditions. That is, each subject is measured under all treatments or treatment combinations. Therefore, Within Subjects designs are sometimes called Repeated Measures designs. Examples of Within designs are S'A, S'AB, S'ABC', etc. Note that these designs involve only factorial relationships between factors, with repeated measures on every treatment. An S'A(B) design also qualifies as a Within design, even though A is nested in B, because subjects are measured under all AB factor combinations. That is, S' is crossed with A and with B.

In a <u>Mixed</u> design, subjects are both nested and crossed with other factors. That is, a Mixed design has both between-subject and within-subject components. Examples are $S'(A)B$, $S'(AB)C$, $S'(A)BC$, $S'(A(B))C$, etc. In the $S'(A)B$ design, A is the between-subject factor and B the within-subject factor; in $S'(A)BC$, A is the between-subject factor while B and C are the within-subject factors; in $S'(A'(B))C$, A and B are between-subject factors and C is the within-subject factor. Thus, in reference to the S' factor, "between" is synonymous with nesting relationships and "within" is synonymous with crossing relationships.

Some cases of Mixed designs are particularly instructive. Consider an $S'(AB'(C))D$ design. Say we want to test the efficacy of two methods of teaching reading, a whole-word vs. a phonetic approach, and to determine if these two methods have differential effects as a function of intelligence. We randomly select four elementary schools from a large city, and separate grade one children into low and high intelligence categories. Twenty children are randomly selected from each of these two categories at each school. Children from two of the schools are taught using the whole-word approach, and the phonetic method is used with the children at the other two schools. All students are taught reading under their respective methods for three school years. At the end of each school year, they are administered a standard reading test so that three reading test scores are obtained for each student. This design can be symbolized $S'_{20}(I_2 H'_2(M_2))Y_3$ where I is intelligence, H' is school, M is method, and Y is school year. Table 1.8 illustrates the $S'_{20}(I_2 H'_2(M_2))Y_3$ design. If half of the students in each school in each intelligence category underwent the phonetic method and half the whole-word method, schools would not be nested in methods, and the design would then be $S'_{10}(I_2 H'_4 M_2)Y_3$. Note that in both designs the total number of subjects employed (160) and the total number of observations (480) is the same.

Table 1.8

An $S'_{20}[I_2H'_2(M_2)]Y_3$ Design

			Y_1	Y_2	Y_3
		i_1	$\begin{matrix}s_1\\ \cdot\\ s_{20}\end{matrix}$	—————————————————————————————————>
	h_1				
		i_2	$\begin{matrix}s_{21}\\ \cdot\\ s_{40}\end{matrix}$	—————————————————————————————————>
m_1					
		i_1	$\begin{matrix}s_{41}\\ \cdot\\ s_{60}\end{matrix}$	—————————————————————————————————>
	h_2				
		i_2	$\begin{matrix}s_{61}\\ \cdot\\ s_{80}\end{matrix}$	—————————————————————————————————>
		i_1	$\begin{matrix}s_{81}\\ \cdot\\ s_{100}\end{matrix}$	—————————————————————————————————>
	h_3				
		i_2	$\begin{matrix}s_{101}\\ \cdot\\ s_{120}\end{matrix}$	—————————————————————————————————>
m_2					
		i_1	$\begin{matrix}s_{121}\\ \cdot\\ s_{140}\end{matrix}$	—————————————————————————————————>
	h_4				
		i_2	$\begin{matrix}s_{141}\\ \cdot\\ s_{160}\end{matrix}$	—————————————————————————————————>

Finally, another interesting Mixed design is S'(A)B(C). For example, suppose we are interested in the effectiveness of two different kinds of seatbelts, particularly which belt is better for fat vs. skinny people. Some number (n) of fat and skinny dummies might be tested using both kinds of seatbelts with two different randomly selected cars for each seatbelt; a Ford and a Cadillac containing one kind of seatbelt and a Chevrolet and a Chrysler containing another kind of seatbelt. This design can be symbolized as $S'_n(F_2)C'_2(B_2)$, where F is Fatness, C' is Car, and B is Seatbelt. This is read, "S' nested in F repeated across C' nested in B," or, more simply, "S' within F across C' within B." This design is shown in Table 1.9.

Table 1.9

An $S'_n(F_2)C'_2(B_2)$ Design

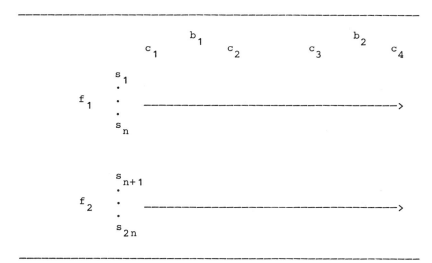

That concludes the chapter. You should now have a firm grasp of some basics of designs. We have discussed most of the designs that are treated in most texts on design. For example, Myers (1979) has seven chapters on designs, of which six are handled by the General Notation System. Much of the chapter is summarized in the three tables that follow. These tables should be studied carefully. Having done this, the exercises at the end of the chapter should be completed.

Table 1.10

How to Read the General Notation System

1. The notation is read from left to right.

2. The symbol S' always refers to the subject factor and always appears in the leftmost position in a design notation. Subsequent symbols such as A, B, C, etc. refer either to treatment factors or to pseudo factors.

3. Each symbol is related to the other symbols by crossing or by nesting. No other relationships are possible. As a consequence, no symbol is isolated from the other symbols in its notation.

4. If a symbol (e.g., Y) is to the immediate left of a symbol (e.g., A) which is enclosed in parentheses, then Y is nested in A. This relationship can be symbolized as Y(A). If Z is in turn nested in A, i.e., Z(A), then Y is nested in Z(A) and ultimately nested in A, the ultimate nesting factor. This relationship can be symbolized as Y(Z(A)). Since Y is nested in Z, and Z is nested in A, then Y is doubly nested. Clearly, triple, quadruple, etc. nestings are also possible. Thus, it is necessary to look at the most inclusive (outermost) parentheses to determine the nesting factor(s). Finally, all nesting relationships are asymmetrical in that if Y is nested in Z, then Z cannot be nested in Y.

5. If a symbol is not nested in another symbol, then it is <u>crossed</u> with it. Thus, a symbol is crossed with the factor to its <u>immediate right</u> if the factor to the right is <u>not</u> enclosed in parentheses. For example, factors A and B are crossed in AB and in (A)B. In these examples, A is necessarily crossed with any other factors to its right.

All crossing relationships are <u>symmetrical</u> in that if A is crossed with B, then B is crossed with A. Any symbol with which the S' factor is crossed represents a <u>repeated measure</u> factor.

6. A prime marker (') above a factor symbol indicates that the factor is <u>random</u>. A symbol without the prime marker represents a <u>fixed</u> factor. In this book, the subject factor and any pseudo factors are always random.

7. The <u>subscript</u> of a nested factor indicates the number of <u>different</u> levels of that factor within <u>each</u> level of its nesting factor. The total number of levels of a nested factor is obtained by multiplying its subscript by the subscript(s) for its nesting factor(s). The subscript of a crossed factor indicates the number of levels of that factor that occur at every level of the other crossed factors. The number of different factor level combinations created by crossing is obtained by multiplying the subscripts of the crossed factors.

8. The total number of observations in an experiment is obtained by multiplying all of the symbol subscripts.

Table 1.11

Relationships Between Factors[1] in Various Designs

Design Type	Factors	Relationship
Between		
S'(A)	S' & A	S' nested in A
S'(AB)	S' & AB	S' nested in AB
	A & B	crossed
S'(A'(B))	S' & A'(B)	S' nested in A'(B)
	A' & B	A' nested in B
S'(AB'(C))	S' & AB'(C)	S' nested in AB'(C)
	A & B'(C)	crossed
	A & C	crossed
	B' & C	B' nested in C
Within		
S'A	S' & A	crossed
S'AB	S' & A	crossed
	S' & B	crossed
	A & B	crossed
S'A'(B)	S' & A'	crossed
	S' & B	crossed
	A' & B	A' nested in B
S'A'(B'(C))	S' & A'	crossed
	S' & B'	crossed
	S' & C	crossed
	A' & B'(C)	A' nested in B'(C)
	A' & C	A' nested in C
	B' & C	B' nested in C

[1]Not to be confused with possible sources of variance

Table 1.11 (cont.)

Design Type	Factors	Relationship
Mixed		
S'(A)B	S' & A	S' nested in A
	S' & B	crossed
	A & B	crossed
S'(AB)C	S' & AB	S' nested in AB
	S' & C	crossed
	A & B	crossed
	A & C	crossed
	B & C	crossed
S'(A'(B))C	S' & A'(B)	S' nested in A'(B)
	S' & C	crossed
	A' & B	A' nested in B
	A' & C	crossed
	B & C	crossed
S'(A)B(C)	S' & A	S' nested in A
	S' & B(C)	crossed
	S' & C	crossed
	A & B(C)	crossed
	A & C	crossed
	B & C	B nested in C

Table 1.12

Guidelines for Constructing Design Diagrams

There are only a few feasible ways to diagram experimental designs. In what follows we offer some guidelines to simplify and standardize the task. Think of the end product, the design diagram, as a matrix of rows and columns. For each level of an experimental factor there is one corresponding row or column.

1. First, enter all between-subject factors in columns. If there are no such factors, skip to Step 2.

   a. Start with the rightmost between-subject factor in the notation and put it to the left on the diagram.

For example, in an $S'_{10}(A'_2(B_3))C_2(D_3)$ design, the rightmost between-subject factor is B. So we list the three levels of B in a single column as:

$$b_1$$
$$b_2$$
$$b_3$$

b. Proceeding left in the notation, find the next between-subject factor and put it on the next column to the right. Do the same for any remaining between-subject factors.

In the illustrative design, A' is the next between-subject factor. Since it is nested in B, we enter two levels of A' for each level of B as:

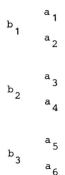

c. For Between-Subjects designs that contain only crossed treatment factors, these factors can be entered on both rows and columns.

2. <u>Enter the subject factor in a column.</u> The column should be the next column to the right of the last factor entered.

For our design, the diagram now looks like this:

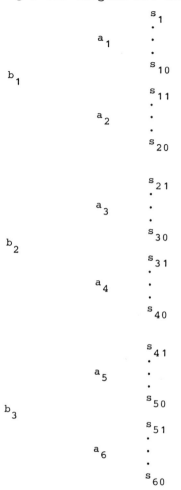

3. <u>Enter all within-subject factors in rows on the</u>
   <u>right side of the diagram.</u>

   a. Begin with the rightmost within-subject factor
       in the design and make this factor the top row.

       In the $S'_{10}(A'_2(B_3))C_2(D_3)$ design, the rightmost
       within-subject factor is D, which is entered
       into the diagram as:

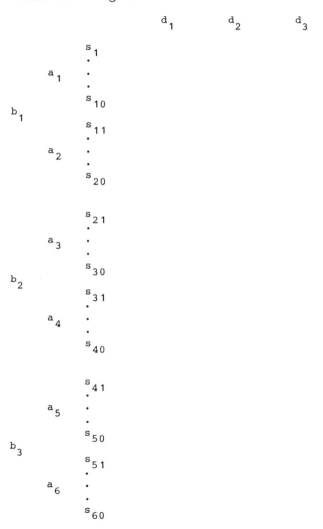

b. Enter any adjacent within-subject factor on the next lowest row (and so on for any remaining within-subject factors).

In our example, the next within-subject factor is C. Since it is nested in D, it is entered as:

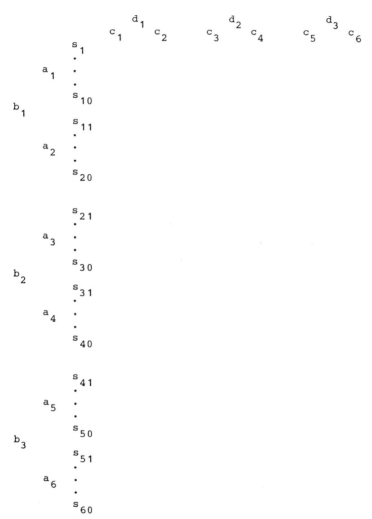

c. Draw arrows from the subject factor across the columns beneath the within-subject factors.

The final diagram for the $S'_{10}(A'_2(B_3))C_2(D_3)$ design is:

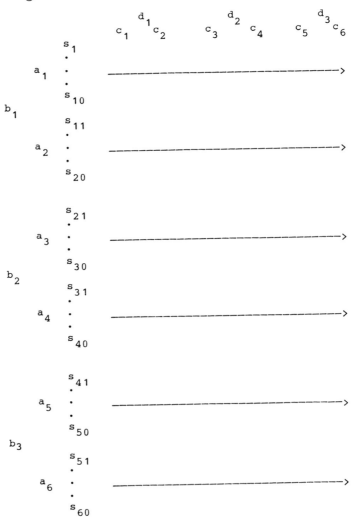

The above diagram shows that there are:

a. Two between-subject factors, B and A'.

b. Two different levels of A' nested in each level of B.

c. Ten different subjects nested in each of the six A'B combinations.

d. Two within-subject factors, C and D.

e. Two different levels of C nested in each level of D.

f. Six different CD treatment combinations to which every subject is exposed. Thus there are 360 or 6 x 60 observations.

EXERCISES

Except for Chapter 5, all of the exercises in this book are based on the designs indicated below. For Chapter 1, the reader's task is to:

(a) diagram the design

(b) determine the total number of subjects

(c) determine the number of levels of a pseudo factor, if any

(d) determine the total number of observations.

The answers to the even numbered problems are given in Appendix·B.

1. $S'_8(A_3)$

2. $S'_5(A_2B_3C_2)$

3. $S'_{12}(A'_3(B_2))$

4. $S'_{10}A_3$

5. $S'_4A_2B_3C_4$

6. $S'_7A'_2(B_3)$

7. $S'_6(A_4)B_3$

8. $S'_3(A_3B_2)C_2$

9. $S'_{10}(A'_3(B'_3))C_4$

10. $S'_5[U'_2(B_2)]T'_2(A_3)$

2

ANALYSIS OF VARIANCE

Behavioral experiments are aimed at determining how one variable influences another. Usually the experimenter exposes some subjects to one or more levels of an <u>independent variable</u> and then measures the effect of this exposure on a <u>dependent variable</u>. For example, suppose researcher M is interested in how lack of sleep affects the ability to drive a car at high speeds. M randomly assigns 10 subjects to each of 3 groups. One group of subjects, the control group, is allowed a full night's sleep. A second group sleeps 4 hours and the third group is kept awake an entire night. In the morning all of the subjects take a high speed driving test. Each subject gets a driving score and for each group a mean driving score is calculated. If lack of sleep influences the ability to drive at high speeds, then the mean driving scores for the three groups should be different, and M can claim that there is an effect of sleep deprivation on driving ability.

The question is how different the groups' means have to be to claim that sleep reliably affects driving ability. Well, how close can we expect the means to be if the amount of sleep had no effect on driving? Surely we cannot expect them to be equal even then, since it is extremely unlikely that 30 people would get the same score on the driving test. If we combine the 30 driving scores and calculate a grand mean, then this mean would be the mean score that any one group might be expected to get. The <u>grand mean</u> would be the best guess about any group's driving ability. If we compute the difference between the obtained group means (i.e., the means based on actual data), and the expected group mean, or grand mean, then each of these differences represents the effect of some amount of lack of sleep on the ability to drive at high speeds. In other words, M tests the obtained differences between the group means against the differences that might arise from chance alone. If the obtained differences are substantially larger than chance, M has evidence of a real <u>effect</u>.

To see if the amount of sleep affected driving performance, M could use several t tests and compare the differences between every possible pair of means. In M's experiment only three such tests would be necessary. But what if there were four or five groups? Since the number of t tests necessary to test all possible pairs of means increases rapidly as the number of means to be compared increases, it would be advantageous to use a statistical procedure that compared all the differences simultaneously. Moreover, in the t test procedure each group mean would be involved in several tests, so the tests would not be independent of each other and conclusions based on outcomes of the tests might be invalid. The analysis of variance procedure circumvents both of these problems by simultaneously and independently comparing the differences between several means.

THE LOGIC OF THE HYPOTHESIS TEST

M wants to make a coherent statement about a full night's sleep, 4 hours of sleep, or no sleep at all and the ability to drive at high speeds. She has a driving score for each subject, a mean driving score for each group, and a grand mean driving score for all groups and all subjects. To claim that sleep affects driving, M needs to be confident that the differences between the group means are a result of her treatment, that is, the amount of sleep the subjects had, and that they are not due to differences between subjects, or different driving courses, test cars, weather conditions, etc. She can control for possible effects of some of these factors easily enough, by using a single car and course for instance, and testing only on clear dry days. If every subject is tested in the same car under the same conditions, then the difference between driving scores cannot be attributed to cars, weather, etc. Unfortunately, in this study M cannot control for subject differences by using the same subject in all conditions. However, if she randomly assigns subjects to treatment groups, then there ought to be as many good and poor drivers in one group as in another so that the subject differences would even out across groups. Then even though it is extremely unlikely that 30 people would get the same score, despite being tested in a single car on a single course, etc., theoretically the group means ought to be equal if there are no treatment effects. Practically speaking though, they will not be identical because each subject's driving score is also affected by characteristics peculiar to that subject and by various other sources of random error.

In order to continue with the hypothesis testing procedure, M needs to make several assumptions. She is actually interested in saying something about anyone who might have had 4 hours of sleep, or no sleep, or a full night's sleep, and his ability to drive. She is not just interested in the subjects that happen to be in her experiment. The first assumption M makes, therefore, is that each of the samples of 10 subjects is a microcosm of the treatment population of potential subjects from which it was selected. This will be true as long as the samples are randomly selected. Then, any conclusions about sleep and driving based on the samples will also be true of their respective treatment populations. M also assumes that, if the samples are large enough, the idiosyncracies of individual subjects will fall out in the wash. That is, when the treatment populations are considered as wholes, these idiosyncracies, or random errors as they are usually called since they also include factors of the experiment peculiar to each subject, will have a mean of zero. In M's experiment, there ought to be as many exceptionally good drivers as exceptionally poor ones, as many deft drivers as clumsy ones, etc., in any treatment group. The third assumption M makes is that these treatment populations have identical means. This makes good intuitive sense if there are as many idiosyncratic subjects in one population as another, and if the particular treatments assigned to the populations are ineffective. In other words, M assumes that in the absence of a treatment effect the means of the treatment populations are equal. And finally, she assumes as a jury might, that the treatments are ineffective, i.e., they do not influence the treatment population means, until shown otherwise.

With these assumptions in mind, M sets up the hypotheses she wants to test. First, she develops her research hypotheses -- mutually exclusive statements about how the experimental factors might relate to the dependent variable. In M's experiment the treatments either influence driving or they do not and M wants to

41

demonstrate the former. So, according to the last assumption, she sets up a <u>null hypothesis</u> and attempts to disconfirm it. Since she wants to demonstrate that the treatments are effective, her <u>null research hypothesis</u> is that the treatments are not, in fact, effective. If she can disconfirm the null hypothesis, then the only alternative is that the treatments do influence driving -- this hypothesis is called the <u>alternative hypothesis</u>. In other words, M decides on a null hypothesis she wants to disconfirm and an alternative hypothesis she wants to support. Since the two are mutually exclusive, if she can disconfirm the null, then she can accept the alternative.

For each research hypothesis M writes, there is a corresponding <u>statistical hypothesis</u>. The assumption that the treatments do not influence driving (i.e., the null hypothesis) is tantamount to asserting that the means of the treatment populations from which the samples were chosen are equal. If we use H_0 to indicate the null hypothesis and the Greek letter μ (mu) to indicate treatment population means, then the <u>statistical null hypothesis</u> can be written as:

$$H_0: \quad \mu_1 = \mu_2 = \mu_3$$

where the subscripts 1, 2, and 3 indicate the control, 4 hours of sleep, and no sleep groups, respectively, in M's experiment.

The research alternative hypothesis states that the treatments do affect driving. The corresponding <u>statistical alternative hypothesis</u> then is that the treatment population means are not equal. This can be written as:

$$H_1: \quad \mu_1 \neq \mu_2 \neq \mu_3$$

where H_1 indicates the alternative hypothesis and the μs are again the treatment population means.

How can M decide whether the null hypothesis or the alternative describes the relationship between sleep and driving ability? We have said that the differences between means are always due in part to experimental error. But if treatment effects are present, then some of the difference is due to them as well. How can M separate these effects? How can the part of the difference due to treatments be estimated separately from the part due to experimental error?

BREAK UP OF SUM OF SQUARES

Consider first the total error in estimating any subject's driving score. We have already stated that the grand mean is the best guess about any score, though we do not expect subjects to get this exact score. The difference between a subject's score and the grand mean is the total error for that subject. Some of it is due to experimental error and some may be due to a treatment effect. To get an estimate of the total error in the experiment, that is, the error for all subjects and all groups, it might seem like a good idea to sum the total errors for each subject. But notice that these separate errors are actually deviations from a mean. Since the sum of any set of deviation scores taken around a mean is zero, this estimate of total error would equal zero. To avoid this problem the deviation scores are squared before summing. The resulting quantity is called the Total Sum of Squares (SS_T) since it is a sum of all the squared deviation scores and since it contains estimates of experimental error and treatment effects. The total sum of squares is written as

$$SS_T = \Sigma (X - \overline{X}_G)^2 \tag{2.1}$$

where X represents each score, $\overline{X}_G$ represents the grand mean, and Σ indicates that the squared deviations should be summed. The total sum of squares provides the key for determining which hypothesis accurately describes the relationship between sleep and driving ability because it can be divided into two independent estimates of the two error components. In other words, the total sum of squares can be decomposed as follows:

$$\Sigma (X - \overline{X}_G)^2 = \Sigma (X - \overline{X}_T)^2 + \Sigma (\overline{X}_T - \overline{X}_G)^2 \tag{2.2}$$

The first quantity to the right of the equal sign, $\Sigma (X - \overline{X}_T)^2$, is called the Within-Groups Sum of Squares (SS_W) since it estimates the amount by which scores within each group differ from their group (treatment) mean ($\overline{X}_T$). The within-groups sum of squares is the estimate of experimental error that M has been looking for.

Since all the subjects in each group were treated alike, the differences between a subject's score (X), and its group or treatment mean ($\overline{X}_T$) will not be affected by different treatments. If we square and sum these differences, the resulting quantity will only estimate the error due to individual differences and uncontrolled factors in the experiment. The within-groups sum of squares can be written as:

$$SS_W = \Sigma(X-\overline{X}_T)^2 \qquad (2.3)$$

$$= \text{experimental error}$$

The second quantity to the right of the equal sign in equation 2.2 is called the Between-Groups Sum of Squares (SS_B), since it estimates the amount the treatment means ($\overline{X}_T$) deviate from the grand mean ($\overline{X}_G$). The between-groups sum of squares is the estimate of treatment effects that M needs to decide between the null and alternative hypotheses. Note that since the experimental errors always affect the group means, the between-groups sum of squares will never be a pure estimate of the treatment effects. It will always contain some influence of experimental error. When the null hypothesis of no treatment effects is true, the between-groups sum of squares will estimate only experimental error since the difference between group means will not be due to treatment effects. If the null hypothesis is false, then the group means will reflect this since the treatment theoretically affects all subjects in a group in a constant fashion. Then the between-groups sum of squares will contain a component due to experimental error and a component due to treatment effects. Thus, when the null hypothesis is true, the between-groups sum of squares can be written as:

$$\text{If } H_o: SS_B = \Sigma(\overline{X}_T-\overline{X}_G)^2 \qquad (2.4)$$

$$= \text{experimental error}$$

If the null hypothesis is false then the SS_B estimates:

$$\text{If } H_1: SS_B = \Sigma(\overline{X}_T-\overline{X}_G)^2 \qquad (2.5)$$

$$= \text{experimental error + treatment effect}$$

The total sum of squares will always equal the sum of the between- and within-groups sums of squares, i.e.,

$$SS_T = SS_B + SS_W \qquad (2.6)$$

regardless of whether the null hypothesis is true.

It is also possible to divide these sums of squares by their respective degrees of freedom (df), -- the number of independent deviation scores on which each is based. The resulting quantities are called mean squares since they are averages or means of squared deviations. Each of these mean squares is an unbiased estimate of its respective error variance. That is, in the long run they yield values the means of which equal the actual population parameter that they estimate. M can compute a total mean square, a between-groups mean square, and a within-groups mean square. The first estimates the average amount of deviation due to experimental error and treatment effect. The second estimates the average amount of deviation due to experimental error and, if the null hypothesis is false, contains an estimate of the average treatment effect as well. The third estimates the average deviation due to experimental error alone.

At last M has a simple mechanism for deciding between the null and alternative hypotheses: she can make a ratio of the between-groups and within-groups mean squares. If the null hypothesis is true, then the ratio should equal 1 since in this case the two mean squares are unbiased estimates of the same thing. Combining equations 2.3 and 2.4 we get:

$$\text{If } H_0: \frac{SS_B}{SS_W} = \frac{\text{experimental error}}{\text{experimental error}} \qquad (2.7)$$

If the null hypothesis is false and if, as is the convention, the between-groups mean square is the numerator, then the ratio should be greater than 1, since in this case the between-groups mean square estimates the treatment effect and experimental error. Combining equations 2.3 and 2.5 we get:

$$\text{If } H_1: \frac{SS_B}{SS_W} = \frac{\text{experimental error + treatment}}{\text{experimental error}} \qquad (2.8)$$

This leads to the conclusion that evidence for treatment effects is obtained when the ratio, called F, is greater than 1. It would be hasty though to leave it at that. Just as we cannot expect all of the subjects to get identical driving scores in the absence of any treatment effects, practically speaking we cannot expect the two estimates to be identical in the absence of treatment effects. This presents a new problem: How much greater than 1 does F have to be for the researcher to assume that the treatments did influence the group means? This question is considered in the next section.

THE F TEST

Recall that we are interested in determining how much of the total sum of squares is due to experimental error and how much is due to treatment effect. We have seen that the within-groups mean square always estimates the average experimental error and, when the null hypothesis is true, the between-groups mean square also estimates this variance. By forming a ratio of the between-groups mean square to the within-groups mean square, M has an index of the variance due to treatments. What she needs is a way to evaluate this ratio.

Assume that the three samples in M's study were in fact selected randomly from the same population (i.e., the H_o is true), and that M computed the two independent estimates of experimental error. If she sampled from this population an indefinite number of times, each time drawing three groups of 10 subjects each and computing an F ratio, she could plot these F's as a function of their probability of occurrence. The shape of the resulting distribution would depend on the number of subjects in each sample as well as the number of samples, in this case 10 and 3 respectively. Intuitively, it should be clear that as the value of F increases, the likelihood of obtaining such a value decreases. At some point an F value will be reached such that chances are only 5 in 100 that it would occur if the groups had been randomly selected from the same population. In other words, there is a value of F such that if the null hypothesis is true, it is very unlikely that an obtained ratio of mean squares will exceed that value. That value is called the critical F value and it depends on the size and number of samples being tested and on how the experimenter defines "unlikely." In psychology, most experimenters acknowledge that an event that occurs 5 times in 100 chances is unlikely, although some prefer 25 in 1000 and others 1 in 100. The level of chance an experimenter picks is called the probability level, or the alpha level, or the significance level. Thankfully, F values at several probability levels have been tabled. An F table is provided in Appendix A.

To evaluate her obtained F value M chooses an alpha level and then finds the intersection of the row and column that corresponds to the df of the within- and between-groups mean squares, respectively. In M's study the within-groups df is 27 since the within-groups mean square is based on 27 independent deviations (see Chapter 4). The between-groups df is 2 since the between-groups mean square is based on 2 independent deviation scores. The F value that appears at the intersection of the column labeled 2 and the row labeled 27 at an alpha level of .05 is 3.35. If M's obtained F ratio equals or exceeds this value, then the probability that the treatment groups came from a single population is less than .05. M can reject the null hypothesis and legitimately claim that the amount of sleep a subject had affected his/her driving ability.

Recall that in order for the F test to be appropriate M must make several assumptions about her data. In addition to those already mentioned, M must also assume that the experimental errors, (i.e., $X - \bar{X}_T$) in each treatment population are distributed normally, that they are independent of each other, and that their variances are equal across treatment populations. If these and the previous assumptions are met, then the F test can be used.

How do violations of the new assumptions affect the utility of the F test? If the experimental errors are not distributed normally it is still possible to use the F test, provided the sample size is large and the groups contain equal numbers of subjects (Keppel, 1973). It is also possible to use the F test when the variances of the experimental errors are not equal, as long as the samples are of equal size (Keppel, 1973). However, in pure Between-Subjects designs such as M's study, if the errors are not independent then the treatment effects and the error effects are confounded, so that their contributions cannot be assessed independently. In Between designs the errors must be independent. For example, suppose M had included mothers and daughters within her treatment groups. Because they are related, we would expect their driving scores to be more similar than the driving scores of two randomly selected individuals. If M got a significant effect for groups, she would not be able to determine if it was attributable to her treatments, or to something peculiar about the way mothers and daughters responded to them. For a more detailed discussion of assumptions and the robustness of the F test see Gaito (1973) or Keppel (1973).

ALPHA AND BETA ERRORS

In selecting her alpha level, M is asserting that an event that occurs with a probability equal to or less than alpha is unlikely. Then if such an improbable event does occur, M claims that its occurrence is not due to chance and she rejects the null hypothesis. Unfortunately, it is possible to follow the entire hypothesis testing procedure correctly, to compute an F, and reject the null hypothesis based on the appropriate tabled value, and be wrong about claiming evidence for a treatment effect. The probability of rejecting the null hypothesis when in fact there is no treatment effect (i.e., when the null hypothesis is true) is alpha. Since M set her alpha level at .05, then 5 times in 100 she might obtain by chance alone an F value greater than the critical F. In such cases, it would be a mistake to reject the null. A Type I or Alpha Error is committed if the researcher rejects the null hypothesis when there are no treatment effects. The probability of a Type I error is alpha.

M can also make a mistake if she obtains an value less than the tabled value and does not reject the null hypothesis. In other words it is possible, though unlikely, to obtain an F less than the critical F when in fact treatment effects do exist. In such a case, M should reject the null hypothesis. The problem is that neither she nor anyone else can identify these situations. Failing to reject the null hypothesis when treatment effects exist is called a Type II or <u>Beta Error</u>. The probability of such an error depends on the alpha level and the magnitude of the true treatment effect. Usually it is impossible to tell whether one of these two errors has occurred. If similar experiments show the same results, then the researcher can be confident that the findings were not due to chance.

WHAT'S IN A SCORE?

Recall that the difference between any single score and the grand mean is attributable to treatment effects, if they exist, and experimental error. It is possible to write this as an equation as follows:

$$(X - \overline{X}_G) = (X - \overline{X}_T) + (\overline{X}_T - \overline{X}_G) \qquad (2.9)$$

where $(X - \overline{X}_G)$ is the difference between any score X and the grand mean $(\overline{X}_G)$. $(X - \overline{X}_T)$ is the difference between a score and the mean of the group or treatment that it is in, and $(\overline{X}_T - \overline{X}_G)$ is the difference between X's treatment mean and the grand mean. The first quantity to the right of the equal sign estimates experimental error and the second estimates any treatment effects. These two components contribute to the value of the deviation of an individual score from the grand mean. With some algebra, we can see what contributes to the value of an individual score:

$$(X - \overline{X}_G) = (X - \overline{X}_T) + (\overline{X}_T - \overline{X}_G)$$
$$X = \overline{X}_G + (X - \overline{X}_T) + (\overline{X}_T - \overline{X}_G) \qquad (2.10)$$

Equation 2.10 indicates that any score is made up of some component due to its population, plus a component due to experimental error, plus a component due to its treatment. A more conventional notation of equation 2.10 is:

$$X = \mu + \alpha + \varepsilon \qquad (2.11)$$

where μ is $\overline{X}_G$, α is $(\overline{X}_T - \overline{X}_G)$, and ε is $(X - \overline{X}_T)$.

Equations 2.10 and 2.11 mean exactly the same thing and are called score models. They indicate the components thought to influence a score. In M's experiment the μ is analogous to the grand mean driving score, the α to the difference between a score's treatment mean and the grand mean, and the ε to the individual and experimental error or the difference between a subject's driving score and the mean of the group that it is in.

Recall that under the null hypothesis the treatment effects are assumed to be zero. Then the appropriate representation of a score is:

$$\text{If } H_o: X = \mu + \varepsilon \qquad (2.12)$$

If there is no experimental error either, then the score model is simply:

$$X = \mu \qquad (2.13)$$

which is one reason why the grand mean is the best guess about a score in the absence of any other knowledge.

We have considered only a simple analysis of variance design with one independent variable. More complex designs are certainly possible and score models can be written for each of them. Regardless of the design, the components that enter into a score model are determined by the experimenter's conceptualization of how the experimental factors affect the dependent measure. For example, in an S'(AB) design there are two treatment factors, each of which potentially influences the dependent variable, so both will appear in the score model. It is possible that two or more factors may interact such that the influence of one factor will depend on the particular level of the other factor(s). In such cases, the experimenter may wish to postulate a potential interaction between the treatment factors. This would be entered in the score model as:

$$X = \mu + \alpha + \beta + \alpha\beta + \varepsilon \qquad (2.14)$$

where μ is the effect of the population, α is the A treatment effect, β is the B treatment effect, $\alpha\beta$ is the AB interaction effect, and ε is experimental error.

As in the simple model, each treatment factor or interaction of factors contributes some amount to the deviation of an individual score from the grand mean, and therefore is associated with some mean square. But mean squares are actually variances, so these treatment factors and combinations of factors are usually referred to as sources of variance. In an S'(AB) design the sources of variance are A, B, an AB interaction, and error variance. In general, the analysis of variance procedure analyzes the contribution various sources of variance make to the total deviation of individual scores from the grand mean.

FIXED VERSUS RANDOM EFFECTS

The foregoing discussion, from a statistical point of view, is concerned with a fixed effects model of analysis of variance. In this model an experimenter selects particular levels of the treatment variable. M chose a full night's sleep, 4 hours of sleep, and no sleep because of some unspecified interest in those particular values. Generally, a researcher using a fixed effects model chooses levels of an independent variable that have some theoretical significance. Sometimes he/she may choose these values because they are all possible values of the independent variable. In any case, with a fixed effects model the researcher is limited to drawing conclusions only about the levels of the independent variable actually included in the study. A significant F ratio in a fixed effects model indicates that some or all of the levels included affected the dependent measure, but it cannot reveal anything about the potential effects of the levels of the independent variables that were not included in the study.

In a random effects model the researcher asks a different question than in the fixed effects model. Whereas in the latter she/he wanted to know if a particular level of some treatment factor influenced the dependent measure, in a random effects model she/he wants to know if there is variability in the way members of some population affect the dependent measure. For example, in many studies several experimenters administer treatments and measure the dependent variable. It is quite possible that the particular experimenter a subject encounters will influence his/her performance. It might be of interest, depending on the study, to determine if changes in the dependent measure are in fact due to such random factors rather than to the effect of the treatments per se. A cognitive researcher interested in two methods of teaching reading (a fixed effect) may want to consider which teacher (a random effect) is conducting the lessons. She/he randomly selects several teachers and each teacher conducts reading class according to both of the approaches. The experimenter is interested in making some statements about which method is more appropriate, regardless of the teacher. The random effects model allows generalizations to be made about the entire population from which the sample was chosen, here across teachers. This model assumes that it is possible to identify every member of the population and select randomly from them. A significant $\underline{F}$ ratio in a random effects model indicates that different "levels" of some population affect the dependent measure differently. Despite the fact that random factors are usually included to increase generalizability (as in the example above), it is also possible to have a genuine interest in a random factor.

3

SOURCES OF VARIANCE

Beginning with this chapter, and for the remaining chapters, the discussion will center on concepts that stem directly from the analysis of variance -- sources of variance, degrees of freedom, sums of squares, expected mean squares, and F ratios. The concept of source of variance is basic since the existence and, indirectly, the quantitative values of the other concepts depend on the specification of sources of variance. We are interested in sources of variance because they allow us to directly assess the contribution that the experimental factors make to the dependent measure. However, sources of variance do not come from "out of the blue." Experimental factors and combinations of factors cannot automatically be equated with sources of variance. Sometimes factors are included in a design in such a manner that their contributions cannot be assessed. So while the present chapter focuses on the question of how sources of variance are identified, we need to back up a bit to understand their origin.

From a Martian point of view, most experiments produce a large set of numbers that have to be organized to be made comprehensible. Organization is no easy task because there are a large number of criteria that can be used to classify any set of numbers. Obviously, some classification schemes will be more appropriate than others. An experiment explicitly or implicitly tests a research hypothesis that suggests a particular experimental design. A design is an abstract, schematic arrangement of experimental factors that yields information relevant to the research hypothesis. In other words, a design acts as a classification scheme for the data. This does not mean that one is stuck with a particular design as a means of organizing a set of data. Alternative designs or re-structurings of the data are often justifiable on a post hoc basis.

The main point is that an experimental design is a starting point for the classification of data. Ordinarily the design then serves as a basis for developing a _statistical model_ of the data. It should be clear why the model comes second. The model must be a model of something. Using certain assumptions about the data (e.g., random sampling), a statistical model represents a theory about what sort of variables should contribute to the value of a particular datum, or score, given the design structure of the experiment.

The General Notation System (GNS) is a shorthand statement about the design of an experiment. Because an experimental design serves as a model of how the data can be organized, the GNS also serves this function, but in a symbolic fashion. More generally, the GNS specifies rules that operate on design notation to yield information relevant to the analysis of variance. This chapter describes a simple rule that operates on notations in order to specify sources of variance.

It is sometimes assumed that different experiments involving the same number of factors yield the same sources of variance. This assumption is faulty because the number and type of sources depend on nesting and crossing relationships among experimental factors. For example, designs such as S'AB, S'(AB), S'(A)B, and S'A(B) all have three experimental factors, but the number and type of sources of variance differ somewhat for each design. Thus, sources of variance should be derived prior to experimentation. The sad researcher is one who carries out an experiment only to discover later that a desired source of variance cannot be isolated.

The next section presents a simple rule for identifying sources of variance whose contributions are assessible. Application of this rule is consistent with statistical models of the analysis of variance for designs we have considered. It should be remembered that these models specify the variables that are assumed to contribute to a particular score value. The rule we shall present acts as a stand in for these models.

DERIVATION OF SOURCES OF VARIANCE

In order to identify and isolate sources of variance one should list distinct combinations of experimental factors by first taking them one at a time, e.g., A, B, C; then two at a time, e.g., AB, AC, BC; and so on, up to the number of factors involved. Note that in combining experimental factors we are not interested in the order of the factors: AB and BA, for example, are different names for the same source of variance. Since one is merely the reverse order of the other, in listing sources of variance either AB or BA would be included but not both.

As mentioned previously, whether a source of variance can be isolated is a function of nesting and crossing relationships among the experimental factors. If all factors are crossed, then all possible combinations can be isolated as sources of variance. If some factors are nested, then the number of combinations that can be isolated is reduced. These considerations are made more precise by the Source Rule.

Source Rule: A combination that involves a nested factor must include its nesting factor. All other combinations of factors are allowable.

In other words, crossed factors are "free" but nested factors are "tied to" their nesting factor. A nested factor cannot be isolated as a source of variance -- it must appear with its nesting factor. It is important to remember that the nesting factor refers to the entire set of factors that a particular factor is nested in. To illustrate, consider an S'(AB) design. Which single factors can be isolated as sources of variance? Since the S' factor is nested in AB, it cannot be isolated. However, since A is not nested and neither is B, both can be isolated as sources of variance. Considering factor pairs, we note that S'(A) and S'(B) cannot be isolated because S' is nested in AB, and it is necessary to take the entire nesting factor (here AB) for a nested factor (here, S'). However, AB can be isolated, since all combinations involving only crossed factors (i.e., where no nesting is involved) are permissible sources of variance. Finally, considering factors three at a time, we note that the overall S'(AB) term can be isolated since the nested factor appears with its entire nesting factor.

By contrast, consider an S'AB design. Since none of the factors are nested (i.e., all factors are crossed), all possible combinations can be isolated as sources of variance: S', A, B, S'A, S'B, AB, and S'AB. It should be clear now that crossing yields more allowable sources of variance than nesting.

Now consider an S'(A)B design. Since S' is nested in A, it cannot be isolated. But A and B are not nested, so both factors can be isolated. The S'(A) source is allowable since neither S' nor A is nested in a factor outside the S'(A) term. However, S'B is not allowable even though S' and B are crossed, since S' is nested in, and consequently tied to, A. The AB source is allowable since neither A nor B is nested. Finally, there is the S'(A)B source.

Some designs look terribly complex and confusing as far as sources of variance are concerned. Consider an S'(A'(B(C))) design. Here S' is nested in A'(B(C)), A' is nested in B(C), and B is nested in C. It should be clear that all single factors except C are nested. Therefore, C is the only allowable single factor source of variance. For this reason, the only allowable combination of two factors is B(C) and the only allowable three factor combination is A'(B(C)). Each of these sources is a nesting factor. Sources S', A', and B cannot be isolated because they are tied to the nesting factors A'(B(C)), B(C), and C, respectively. Since the nesting factor refers to the entire set of factors that a particular factor is nested in, sources such as S'(A'), S'(B), S'(C), S'(A'(B)), S'(A'(C)), and S'(B(C)) cannot be isolated since each of these terms contains at least one factor which is nested in a factor not contained in the term of interest.

AIDS IN DERIVING SOURCES OF VARIANCE

The Source Rule is sufficient to generate all allowable sources of variance. However, in multifactor designs it is easy to overlook some sources. In this section some aids are provided that will reduce this possibility.

General Considerations

When deriving sources of variance, care should be taken to clearly identify them by maintaining appropriate parentheses and prime markers ('). For example, in a S'A(B) design, the S'B source is written without parentheses because S' is crossed with B, whereas the variance due to the combination of factors A and B is written A(B), not AB or B(A), since A is nested in B. The S' source is written with the prime. The reasons for these precautions will become clear later on.

Systematic Approach

Sources should be derived in a systematic manner by first considering all single factors or **main effects**, then all two factor combinations or **first-order** interactions, then all three factor combinations or **second-order** interactions, etc. In an S'(A)BC design, taking one factor at a time yields sources A, B, and C; taking two factors at a time yields S'(A), AB, AC, and BC; taking three factors at a time yields S'(A)B, S'(A)C, and ABC; and finally, taking four factors at a time yields S'(A)BC.

Absolute Number of Sources

No general formulas exist for determining how many sources of variance can be isolated in Hierarchical designs since the nesting and crossing relationships characteristic of them are numerous. It is worth noting, however, that the number of sources for pure Hierarchical Between designs is equal to the number of experimental factors in the design -- three sources for an S'(A(B)) design, four for an S'(A(B(C))) design, etc. It is also possible to check sources of variance based on degrees of freedom and such a technique will

be presented in the next chapter. Fortunately, formulas can be derived for determining the number of
sources in non-Hierarchical Between, Within, and Mixed
designs. These are presented below.

In non-Hierarchical <u>Between</u> designs the number of
sources of variance is:

$$2^t$$

where t equals the number of treatment factors. In an
S'(A) design, then, there are 2^1 or 2 sources of
variance. In an S'(AB) design there are 2^2 or 4
sources of variance and in an S'(ABC) design there are
2^3 or 8 sources of variance.

In non-Hierarchical <u>Within</u> designs the number of
sources of variance is:

$$2^f - 1$$

where f equals the number of experimental factors. In
an S'A design there are $2^2 - 1$ or 3 sources of variance.
In an S'AB design there are $2^3 - 1$ or 7 sources of
variance, and in an S'ABC design, $2^4 - 1$ or 15 sources of
variance.

In non-Hierarchical <u>Mixed</u> designs the number of
sources of variance is:

$$2^t + 2^c - 1$$

where t equals the number of treatment factors and c
equals the number of treatment factors crossed with the
subject factor. In an S'(A)B design there are $2^2 + 2^1 - 1$
or 5 sources of variance. In an S'(A)BC design there
are $2^3 + 2^2 - 1$ or 11 sources of variance, and in an
S'(AB)C design there are $2^3 + 2^1 - 1$ or 9 sources of
variance.

<u>Number of Main Effect and Interaction Sources of</u>
<u>Variance</u>

In non-Hierarchical Between designs, when treatment factors are crossed, the number of main effects,
first-order interactions, second-order interactions,
etc., is:

$$\frac{t!}{r!(t-r)!}$$

where t equals the total number of treatment factors and r equals the number of factors in the subset under consideration. Thus r=1 when considering main effects, r=2 when considering first-order interactions, r=3 when considering second-order interactions, etc. With the four treatment factors A, B, C, D, the number of first-order interactions is $4!/[2!(4-2)!]$ or 6 -- AB, AC, AD, BC, BD, and CD. The above formula is also appropriate for non-Hierarchical Within designs if the number of experimental factors is used, rather than the number of treatment factors.

Table 3.1 presents the sources of variance for a representative sample of Hierarchical and non-Hierarchical Between, Within, and Mixed designs. The reader should study this table.

Table 3.1

Sources of Variance in Various Designs

Design Type	Sources of Variance
Between	
S'(A)	A, S'(A)
S'(AB)	A, B, AB, S'(AB)
S'(A'(B))	B, A'(B), S'(A'(B))
S'(AB'(C))	A, C, AC, B'(C), AB'(C), S'(AB'(C))
Within	
S'A	S', A, S'A
S'AB	S', A, B, S'A, S'B, AB, S'AB
S'A'(B)	S', B, S'B, A'(B), S'A'(B)
S'A'(B'(C))	S', C, S'C, B'(C), S'(B'(C)), A'(B'(C)), S'A'(B'(C))
Mixed	
S'(A)B	A, B, S'(A), AB, S'(A)B
S'(AB)C	A, B, C, AB, AC, BC, S'(AB), ABC, S'(AB)C
S'(A'(B))C	B, C, A'(B), BC, S'(A'(B)), A'(B)C, S'(A'(B))C
S'(A)B(C)	A, C, S'(A), AC, B(C), S'(A)C, AB(C), S'(A)B(C)

EXERCISES

Determine the sources of variance for the designs notated in the exercises for Chapter 1. The answers for the even numbered problems are provided in Appendix B.

4

DEGREES OF FREEDOM

The concept of degrees of freedom (df) was mentioned in Chapter 2. Recall that when a mean is computed on a set of n terms, the value of the nth term is determined by the values of the other n-1 terms. That is, the first n-1 terms are free to take on any value, but since the sum of the deviations of the scores from the mean must equal zero, these values constrain the value of the nth term. The number of terms that are free to vary is called the <u>degrees of freedom</u>.

Degrees of freedom are relatively easy to calculate when a set of numbers is only constrained by one mean. The situation readily complicates, however, as the design matrix in which sets of numbers are embedded becomes more complex. That is, as sets of numbers become nested and crossed with other sets of numbers, the number of constraints increases, since the mean of each set constrains the value of one member in its set. In other words, as the number of factors and factor combinations that are assumed to affect a set of scores increases, the number of constraints on what the scores can be also increases. Each constraint on the scores limits the number of scores that are free to vary. Therefore, as the number of constraints increases, the number of free scores or degrees of freedom decreases.

As mentioned in Chapter 2, our interest in df stems from the desire to have several <u>unbiased</u> estimates of the variance due to particular experimental factors. Division of a sum of squares by the appropriate df yields these unbiased estimates. One must know the correct df in order to do this, of course, so it is not surprising that it is at this point that many researchers run to the nearest book on experimental design, hoping to find the appropriate formulas for calculating df. There are such formulas but their mechanical application has little educational value, since the researcher may use them while failing to understand their origin. Because these formulas do not come from out of the blue, this chapter opens with a discussion of df and its relationship to experimental design. Then, since df are directly related to the experimental design, which is symbolized by the General Notation System, a Degrees of Freedom Rule is offered that operates on the system to generate formulas for df.

DEGREES OF FREEDOM IN EXPERIMENTAL DESIGNS

Why do the df for sources of variance have the values they do? It is one thing to understand that the estimation of a simple mean for a set of numbers results in the loss of 1 df for the set. It may come as a surprise, however, that a set of numbers may be constrained by two or more means, each of which may themselves be constrained. This point is elaborated below in a discussion of the "why" of df for sources of variance in representative Within, Between, and Mixed designs.

Df in Within-Subjects Designs

Consider a Within-Subjects design such as $S'_{10}A_2B_3$. In estimating the variance due to each main effect, a single df is lost. Hence, the df associated with the S', A, and B sources of variance are 9, 1, and 2, respectively, since each set of scores is constrained only by the overall (grand, matrix) mean. Here, the scores are actually means. For example, in estimating the variance due to subjects a mean is first computed for each subject across the 6 treatment combinations. Since there are 10 subjects, 9 of these means can assume any value, but the tenth mean in the set can take on only one value owing to the constraint imposed by the mean of the set, in this case the grand mean. The same is true for the A and B sources of variance. Each A mean is computed across the $SB=30$ combinations. Once one of the A means takes on a value, the value of the second mean is already determined. Likewise, the value of the third B mean, computed across the $SA=20$ combinations, is already determined once the first two B means assume a particular value. The nature of this constraint is such that all but one of the means is free to vary. In sum, the 10 S' means, the 2 A means, and the 3 B means each lose one df so that the

$$\text{df for S'} = s-1$$
$$= 10-1$$
$$= 9$$

$$\text{df for A} = a-1$$
$$= 2-1$$
$$= 1$$

$$\text{df for B} = b-1$$
$$= 3-1$$
$$= 2$$

The basis of the df for the two-factor sources in the design is not so obvious. However, a <u>residual method</u> can be used to determine these df (Myers, 1979). In this method, the question is what's left over after the necessary constraints have been removed. This entails determining the total number of values in the design matrix, and then subtracting appropriate constraints as the sources of variance dictate. For example, to determine the df associated with the S'A source, note that the S'A matrix of 20 or 10 X 2 values is initially constrained by the grand mean, so that 1 df is lost. The S' means and the A means also constrain the values in the matrix. However, since these sets of means are themselves constrained by the grand mean, we lose s-1 and a-1 df, rather than s and a df. In other words, there are actually s-1 and a-1 means that also act as constraints on the values in the S'A matrix. (The reader is encouraged to construct such a matrix and confirm this point.) These considerations lead to the conclusion that the df for the S'A source are

$$\text{df for S'A} = (sa-1)-(s-1)-(a-1)$$
$$= (10)(2)-1-(10-1)-(2-1)$$
$$= 9$$

For analogous reasons, the df for the S'B source are

$$\text{df for S'B} = (sb-1)-(s-1)-(b-1)$$
$$= (10)(3)-1-(10-1)-(3-1)$$
$$= 18$$

and the df for the AB source are

$$
\begin{aligned}
\text{df for AB} &= (ab-1)-(a-1)-(b-1) \\
&= (2)(3)-1-(2-1)-(3-1) \\
&= 2
\end{aligned}
$$

In summary tables, these df formulas are usually condensed by factoring to $(s-1)(a-1)$ for the S'A source, $(s-1)(b-1)$ for the S'B source, and $(a-1)(b-1)$ for the AB source. These formulas, while simple and accurate, fail to reveal why df are lost.

Finally, consider the S'AB source of variance in the $S'_{10}A_2B_3$ design. This source can be viewed as a cube matrix S'=10 rows long, A=2 columns wide, and B=3 sections deep. Imposition of the grand mean on the entire matrix results in the loss of 1 df. By a typical score model, the 60 cubicles (i.e., scores) in the matrix are a function of the S', A, and B factors and of their interactions. Hence, the overall S'AB matrix can be seen as constructed from the S'A, S'B, and AB sub-matrices. Each of these sub-matrices reduces the number of scores in the larger S'AB matrix that are free to vary. We know that the S'A term results in a loss of $(sa-1)-(s-1)-(a-1)$ df, the SB term in $(sb-1)-(s-1)-(b-1)$ df, and the AB term in $(ab-1)-(a-1)-(b-1)$ df. Furthermore, the S', A, and B means, each initially constrained by 1 df, also result in the loss of df. The final formula for the S'AB source therefore becomes

$$
\begin{aligned}
\text{df for S'AB} &= (sab-1)-[(sa-1)-(s-1)-(a-1)] - \\
&\quad [(sb-1)-(s-1)-(b-1)] - \\
&\quad [(ab-1)-(a-1)-(b-1)] - \\
&\quad (s-1)-(a-1)-(b-1) \\[6pt]
&= sab-1-sa+1+s-1+a-1-sb+1+s-1+b-1 \\
&\quad -ab+1+a-1+b-1-s+1-a+1-b+1 \\[6pt]
&= sab-sa-sb-ab+s+a+b-1 \\[6pt]
&= 60-20-30-6+10+2+3-1 \\[6pt]
&= 18
\end{aligned}
$$

This formula is usually shortened by factoring to

$$
\text{df for S'AB} = (s-1)(a-1)(b-1)
$$

Df in Between-Subjects Designs

The explanation of df for sources of variance associated with Between-Subjects designs should be easier to understand now. Consider an $S'_{20}(A'_2(B_3))$ design. The B source has 2 or 3-1 df since the B means are only constrained by the grand mean.

Determining the df for the A'(B) source presents a new problem. We have not as yet considered df for sources of variance that involve nesting. While the residual method can be used to obtain these df, it is cumbersome. In determining the df for A'(B), we first note that in an $S'(A'(B))$ design the total between-groups effects are composed of the A'(B) and B effects. NOTE: The $S'(A'(B))$ source reflects the within-groups effect. That is, the total between-groups df equals the df for A'(B)) plus the df for B. Thus, the df for A'(B) equals the total between-groups df minus the df for B. The df for B are b-1, and therefore the

$$df \text{ for } A'(B) = (ab-1)-(b-1)$$
$$= ab-1-b+1$$
$$= ab-b$$
$$= 6-3$$
$$= 3$$

A conceptually simpler way of determining the df for the A'(B) source involves the <u>pooling method</u> (Myers, 1979). To use this method, determine the number of levels of a factor that are nested in its nesting factor, subtract 1 from this number, and then multiply the result by the number of levels of the nesting factor. Thus, for the A'(B) source, there are 2 levels of A nested in each level of B. The B level mean constrains the values of A so that 1 df is lost at each level of AB -- i.e., there are a-1 df at each B level. Since there are b such levels, a-1 is multiplied by b. That is, the a-1 df are pooled across the B levels. This leads to the result that, as for the residual method, the

$$df \text{ for } A'(B) = (a-1)b$$
$$= (2-1)3$$
$$= 3$$

The df for the S'(A'(B)) source can also be obtained by either the pooling or the residual method. From the pooling perspective, this source arises from ab=6 groups, each of which contains s observations. Each of these s observations loses 1 df due to the constraint imposed by the group mean. Since this happens 6 times, the

$$
\begin{aligned}
\text{df for S'(A'(B))} &= (s-1)(ab) \\
&= (19)(6) \\
&= 114
\end{aligned}
$$

Let's try the residual method. The S'(A'(B)) term is the only within-groups source. In determining df, therefore, it can be considered to be what's left over from the total df after the between-groups df have been extracted. Thus we have

$$
\begin{aligned}
\text{df for S'(A'(B))} &= (sab-1)-(ab-1) \\
&= sab-ab \\
&= 120 - 6 = 114
\end{aligned}
$$

Df in Mixed Designs

No new mysteries arise in determining df as we turn to mixed designs. Consider an $S_{20}'(A_3)B_2$ design. The A and B sources are associated with a-1=2 and b-1=1 df, respectively, owing to the single constraint imposed by the grand mean. The S'(A) source has (s-1)a=57 df since, by the pooling method, the s observations in each A level are constrained by that A level mean, and this occurs a times. The residual method can also be used to obtain the df for the S'(A) source. Start by noting that the between-subjects effects are A and S'(A). So the total between-subjects df are as-1, since this is the total number of between-subjects observations minus 1. The df for the A term is a-1. Thus, (as-1)-(a-1) ought to yield the same df for the S'(A) source as the pooling method. Indeed it does, since

$$
\begin{aligned}
\text{df for S'(A)} &= (as-1)-(a-1) \\
&= as-a \\
&= 60-3 \\
&= 57
\end{aligned}
$$

We have already discussed how df are determined for a source such as AB (i.e., (ab-1)-(a-1)-(b-1) = 5-2-1=2, by the residual method). Similarly, the df for the S'(A)B source can be determined by the residual method. The within-subjects effects in an S'(A)B design are B, AB, and S'(A)B, since they all contain a within-subjects component, i.e., a repeated measure. Thus, the S'(A)B effect equals total within-subjects effect minus the B effect minus the AB effect, or analogously, the df for the S'(A)B source can be parceled as

$$\text{df for } S'(A)B = sa(b-1)-(b-1)-(a-1)(b-1)$$
$$= 60(1)-1-(2)(1)$$
$$= 57$$

By the pooling method, the df for S'(A)B are determined by pooling the df in the SB matrix across the levels of A. Thus, the

$$\text{df for } S'(A)B = (s-1)(b-1)(a)$$
$$= (19)(1)(3)$$
$$= 57$$

It should be clear now how df are directly related to the particular design of an experiment. Consequently, we can proceed with the <u>Degrees of Freedom Rule</u>. This rule operates on the General Notation System to yield formulas for df associated with sources of variance that have been generated by the Source Rule.

HOW TO COMPUTE DEGREES OF FREEDOM

The first step in obtaining df formulas is to apply the <u>Source Rule</u> (from Chapter 3) to determine those sources of variance that can be isolated. Once sources of variance have been appropriately listed, it is easy to determine the df associated with each source by using the Degrees of Freedom Rule. This rule generates computational formulas that can be used rather mechanically to obtain the required df.

<u>Degrees of Freedom Rule</u>: For sources of variance without parentheses, subtract 1 from all factor subscripts before multiplying all subscript values. For sources of variance that contain parentheses, subtract 1 from the subscript of any factor that lies outside the <u>outermost</u> parentheses and multiply the product of these values by the subscripts of the factors inside the parentheses.

This rule can be broken down into two cases, one involving sources of variance with crossed factors <u>only</u> and the second involving sources of variance with any nested factors.

If a source of variance contains only crossed factors (i.e., no parentheses), simply subtract 1 from each of the factor subscripts and multiply these obtained values. For example, in an S'(AB) design, the sources of variance that contain only crossed factors are A, B, and AB, and their df are a-1, b-1, and (a-1)(b-1) respectively. It is implicit in this case that for sources of variance involving only a single factor, the df are simply the subscript for that factor minus 1. Thus, the A source from an S'(A) design has a-1 df associated with it. Similarly, the A source has a-1 df in the following designs: S'A, S'(A)B, S'(B(A)), S'(AB)C, and S'AB.

If a source of variance contains nested factors (i.e., parentheses are present), one more step is involved in obtaining df formulas. In this case, subtract 1 from the subscripts of factors <u>outside</u> the <u>most inclusive</u> (outermost) parentheses and multiply the product of these values by the subscripts of all factors inside the parentheses. For example, the

df for an S'(A) source	= (s-1)(a)
for an S'(AB) source	= (s-1)(ab)
for an S'(A)B source	= (s-1)(a)(b-1)
for an A'(B) source	= (a-1)(b)
for an S'(A'(B)) source	= (s-1)(ab)

Note for the S'(A'(B)) source that the most inclusive parentheses are those which surround A' and B. Hence, the A and B subscripts remain intact, but 1 is subtracted from the subscript of that factor, here S', which is outside those parentheses. By analogy, an S'(A(B))C source has (s-1)(ab)(c-1) df.

In Table 4.1, the Degrees of Freedom Rule is illustrated in conjunction with some representative designs. Study this table quite carefully, because it will facilitate completion of the exercises.

Table 4.1

Degrees of Freedom in Some Representative Designs

$S'_{10}(A_4)$

SV	df formula	df
A	a-1	3
S'A	(s-1)a	36
Total	sa-1	39

$S'_8(A_2B_5)$

SV	df formula	df
A	a-1	1
B	b-1	4
AB	(a-1)(b-1)	4
S'(AB)	(s-1)(ab)	70
Total	sab-1	79

$S'_{12}A_3$

SV	df formula	df
S'	s-1	11
A	a-1	2
S'A	(s-1)(a-1)	22
Total	sa-1	35

$S'_5A_6B_3$

SV	df formula	df
S'	s-1	4
A	a-1	5
B	b-1	2
S'A	(s-1)(a-1)	20
S'B	(s-1)(b-1)	8
AB	(a-1)(b-1)	10
S'AB	(s-1)(a-1)(b-1)	40
Total	sab-1	89

Table 4.1 (continued)

$S_7'(A_3)B_2$

SV	df formula	df
A	a−1	2
B	b−1	1
S'(A)	(s−1)a	18
AB	(a−1)(b−1)	2
S'(A)B	(s−1)a(b−1)	18
Total	sab−1	41

$S_6'[A_4'(B_2)]C_3$

SV	df formula	df
B	b−1	1
C	c−1	2
A'(B)	(a−1)b	6
BC	(b−1)(c−1)	2
S'[A'(B)]	(s−1)ab	40
A'(B)C	(a−1)b(c−1)	12
S'[A'(B)]C	(s−1)ab(c−1)	80
Total	sabc−1	143

$S_5'[A_6(B_3)C_2]$

SV	df formula	df
B	b−1	2
C	c−1	1
A(B)	(a−1)b	15
BC	(b−1)(c−1)	2
A(B)C	(a−1)b(c−1)	15
S'[A(B)C]	(s−1)abc	144
Total	sabc−1	179

EXERCISES

Determine the degrees of freedom associated with the sources of variance for the designs indicated in the Chapter 1 exercises. The answers for the even numbered problems are provided in Appendix B.

5

SUMS OF SQUARES AND MEAN SQUARES

This chapter focuses on the numerator portion of a variance estimate, i.e., the sum of squared deviations, more commonly referred to as the "sum of squares." Discussions of sums of squares are often described as "awesome," "forbidding," and the like. The sum of squares formulas look complex and their relationship to other concepts in the analysis of variance is unclear -- so it is said. This chapter attempts to provide the basis for a brighter outlook. The key will be to show how sum of squares formulas can be "read." Then, in keeping with prior chapters, a simple rule, the Sum of Squares Rule, is presented. This Rule simplifies the construction and understanding of sum of squares formulas. Some readers could well ask at this point why such a rule needs to be discussed; after all, don't computer programs do all the computations? Of course, they do just that. But reliance on the computer too often blocks any real understanding of the concepts involved in statistical analysis. So we forge ahead with a discussion of the concept of sum of squares.

THE DEFINITION OF SUM OF SQUARES

By the defining formula, a sum of squares is

$$\Sigma(X-\overline{X})^2 \qquad (5.1)$$

where X represents each score and $\overline{X}$ represents the mean of the X's. Formula 5.1 indicates that the mean of a set is subtracted from each score in the set and the resulting differences are squared and then summed.

In theory, one could calculate sums of squares by using the defining formula. However, computations become tedious even when a few scores must be analyzed. Therefore, a <u>computational formula</u> has been devised that is equivalent to the defining formula but which only uses raw scores, i.e., no prior calculations of means are necessary to determine the sum of squares. With some algebra (see Hays, 1963, p. 371 for the proof) it can be shown that a sum of squares is also equal to:

$$\Sigma(X)^2 - \frac{(\Sigma X)^2}{N} \qquad (5.2)$$

The term on the left (i.e., $\Sigma(X)^2$) indicates that each score is squared and then the squares are summed. The term on the right (i.e., $(\Sigma X)^2/N$) indicates that the scores are summed and then this total is squared and divided by the number of scores summed. Finally, the term on the right is subtracted from the term on the left. Since the computational formulas for sums of squares can become complicated, the section below explains how the formulas can be read.

SIGMAS, SUPERSCRIPTS, AND PARENTHESES

A computational formula is a set of <u>terms</u> that specify which arithmetic operations to <u>perform</u> on certain numbers. The typical formula looks like a maze of subscripts, superscripts, summation signs, and parentheses. This makes them hard to read, especially at first. A few guidelines that stem directly from the General Notation System may make this task easier.

Perhaps the best way to explain how to read formulas is through an example. Table 5.1 presents the analysis of data for an $S_2^1(A_4)$ Between-Subjects design.

Inspection of the Preliminary Summary Table reveals that each sum of squares (SS) computational formula contains two terms, one on either side of the minus sign. Although computational formulas sometimes contain more than two terms, all such formulas are composed of similar terms. Each term is a self-contained entity that provides instructions to operate on certain numbers in a certain way.

A closer look at the computational formulas (whose origin will be explained later) in Table 5.1 reveals some characteristics of all computational formulas: (a) Every term in a computational formula contains a summation sign for each experimental factor in the design; (b) The numerator in each term is divided by the product of the levels of the factor(s) inside the parentheses. This is tantamount to dividing by n and is directly analogous to the n in the general computing formula for the sum of squares (see Formula 5.2); (c) The quantities within parentheses are squared; (d) Each computational formula resembles the general computing formula given in Formula 5.2 above; and (e) Each source of variance is associated with a different computational formula.

Table 5.1

Analysis of Data for an $S'_2(A_4)$ Between-Subjects Design

Preliminary Summary Table

SV	df	Expanded df	SS Computational Formulas
A	$a-1$	$a-1$	$\overset{a}{\Sigma}(\overset{s}{\Sigma}X)^2/s - (\overset{as}{\Sigma\Sigma}X)^2/as$
S'(A)	$(s-1)(a)$	$as-a$	$\overset{as}{\Sigma\Sigma}(X)^2 - \overset{a}{\Sigma}(\overset{s}{\Sigma}X)^2/s$
Total	$as-1$	$as-1$	$\overset{as}{\Sigma\Sigma}(X)^2 - (\overset{as}{\Sigma\Sigma}X)^2/as$

Table 5.1 (continued)

Hypothetical Data

		X	$\overset{s}{\Sigma}X$	$(\overset{s}{\Sigma}X)^2$	$\overset{s}{\Sigma}(X)^2$
a_1	s_1	1	1	1	1+0=1
	s_2	0			
a_2	s_3	1	3	9	1+4=5
	s_4	2			
a_3	s_5	3	8	64	9+25=34
	s_6	5			
a_4	s_7	1	2	4	1+1=2
	s_8	1			

$$\overset{as}{\Sigma\Sigma}X = 14 \qquad \overset{a}{\Sigma}(\overset{s}{\Sigma}X)^2 = 78 \qquad \overset{as}{\Sigma\Sigma}(X)^2 = 42$$

SS Computations

$$SS_A = (78/2)-(14^2/8) = 39-24.5 = 14.5$$

$$SS_{S'(A)} = 42 - 39 = 3$$

$$SS_{TOTAL} = 42 - 24.5 = 17.5$$

Summary Table

SV	df	SS	MS	F	p
A	3	14.50	4.83	6.44	>.05
S'(A)	4	3.00	.75	—	

Note also that there are three distinct kinds of terms in the computational formulas: (1) Some terms have all their summation signs or sigmas <u>outside</u> the parentheses, e.g., $\Sigma\Sigma(X)^2$. Although this kind of term can be presented without parentheses as $\Sigma\Sigma X^2$, we prefer to include them for clarity; (2) Some terms have all their summation signs <u>inside</u> the parentheses, e.g., $(\Sigma\Sigma X)^2$; and (3) Some terms have summation signs both <u>outside and inside</u> the parentheses, e.g., $\Sigma(\Sigma X)$. Terms that have all their sigmas either inside or outside the parentheses need only be computed once, though they may be used repeatedly. Such terms entail a single summation process. Terms that have summation signs both inside and outside the parentheses entail two summation processes.

As indicated earlier, each term necessitates squaring something at some point. If all the sigmas are outside the parentheses, then every score in the data matrix is squared and then the squares are summed. Terms that have all their sigmas inside the parentheses call for summing <u>all</u> the scores in the data matrix and then squaring the total. In general, the sigmas outside the parentheses indicate which scores to sum after squaring and those inside the parentheses indicate which scores to sum before squaring. When sigmas appear both inside and outside the parentheses, the outside sigmas indicate how the initial summation process is restricted. In effect the outside sigmas say, "Sum what's inside the parentheses at each level of me, square these sums, and then sum the resulting squares." The inside sigmas specify which scores to sum at each level or combination of levels indicated by the outside sigmas. For example, $\Sigma(\Sigma X)^2$ indicates that the X's should be summed across the levels of S, separately for each level of A; that the resulting sums should be squared; and then these squares should be summed. The term $\Sigma\Sigma(X)^2$ contains only outside sigmas and indicates that the X at each AS level should be squared. Then these squares should be summed. The term $(\Sigma\Sigma X)^2$ contains only inside sigmas and indicates that all the X's are summed and then this sum is squared.

It takes a while to become familiar with computational formulas and how they apply to a matrix of numbers. We recommend that you study Table 5.1 until you feel comfortable with the formulas. Having done this, you may appreciate the patterns in these formulas.

DETAILS OF SUMS OF SQUARES

Recall that the analysis of variance procedure estimates the variance due to particular experimental factors or combinations of factors, and that the sums of squares are the numerators of these variance estimates. Recall also that the sources of variance that can be isolated in any experiment depend on the structure of the design. So it is possible to analyze a single set of data in various ways, depending on how the design is structured. Table 5.2 presents an $S_2'A_4$ Within-Subjects design using the same data that was analyzed as an $S_2'(A_4)$ Between-Subjects design in Table 5.1.

Table 5.2

Analysis of Data for an $S_2'A_4$ Within-Subjects Design

Preliminary Summary Table

SV	df	Expanded df	SS Computational Formulas
S'	s−1	s−1	$\overset{s}{\Sigma}(\overset{a}{\Sigma}X)^2/a - (\overset{as}{\Sigma\Sigma}X)^2/as$
A	a−1	a−1	$\overset{a}{\Sigma}(\overset{s}{\Sigma}X)^2/s - (\overset{as}{\Sigma\Sigma}X)^2/as$
S'A	(s−1)(a−1)	as−a−s+1	$\overset{as}{\Sigma\Sigma}(X)^2 - \overset{a}{\Sigma}(\overset{s}{\Sigma}X)^2/s$
			$- \overset{s}{\Sigma}(\overset{a}{\Sigma}X)^2/a + (\overset{as}{\Sigma\Sigma}X)^2/as$
Total	(a)(s)−1	as−1	$\overset{as}{\Sigma\Sigma}(X)^2 - (\overset{as}{\Sigma\Sigma}X)^2/as$

Hypothetical Data

	a_1	a_2	a_3	a_4	
s_1	1	1	3	1	$(\overset{a}{\Sigma}X) = 6$
s_2	0	2	5	1	$(\overset{a}{\Sigma}X) = 8$
$(\overset{s}{\Sigma}X)$	1	3	8	2	$\overset{as}{\Sigma\Sigma}X = 14$
$\overset{s}{\Sigma}(X)^2$	1	5	34	2	$\overset{as}{\Sigma\Sigma}(X)^2 = 42$

Table 5.2 (Continued)

Computation of SS

$$SS_{S'} = [(6^2 + 8^2)/4]-(14^2/8) = (100/4) - 24.5 = .5$$

$$SS_A = [(1^2 +3^2 +8^2 +2^2)/2]-24.5 = (78/2) - 24.5 = 14.5$$

$$SS_{S'A} = 42 - 39 - 25 + 24.5 = 2.5$$

$$SS_{TOTAL} = 42 - 24.5 = 17.5$$

Summary Table

SV	df	SS	MS	F	p
S'	3	.50	.17	—	
A	1	14.50	14.50	17.47	<.05
S'A	3	2.50	.83	—	

Since the data are the same, the total sums of squares are equal in the two matrices. The sums of squares for the A treatment factors are also equal. Thus, the computational formulas for SS_{TOTAL} are identical in the two designs, since these sources estimate identical variance components in these two designs.

The difference between the designs is that the variability due to S'(A) in the Between-Subjects design has been parceled into variability due to S' and S'A in the Within-Subjects design. And, as you've probably guessed, since $SS_{S'(A)} = SS_{S'} + SS_{S'A}$, the substitution of the computational formulas into this equation yields an equivalence. That is,

$$\overset{as}{\Sigma\Sigma}(X)^2 - \overset{a}{\Sigma}(\overset{s}{\Sigma}X)^2/s = [\overset{s}{\Sigma}(\overset{a}{\Sigma}X)^2/a - (\overset{as}{\Sigma\Sigma}X)^2/as]$$

$$+ \overset{as}{\Sigma\Sigma}(X)^2 - \overset{a}{\Sigma}(\overset{s}{\Sigma}X)^2/s$$

$$- \overset{s}{\Sigma}(\overset{a}{\Sigma}X)^2/a + (\overset{as}{\Sigma\Sigma}X)^2/as]$$

$$42 - 39 = (25-24.5) + (42-39-25+24.5)$$

$$3 = .5 + 2.5$$

$$3 = 3$$

Thus, it is clear that while the total variability is the same in the two designs, it is divided up differently. The difference is due to the fact that, in the Within-Subjects design, variability due to subjects can be differentiated from that due to the interaction between subjects and treatments. Notice too that the most complex computational formula in Table 5.2 is that for S'A. This formula suggests that assessment of a pure S'A effect requires that variability due to S' and to A must first be removed from their joint effect.

Table 5.3 presents the data analysis for an $S'_2(A_2)B_2$ Mixed design. Once again we have entered the same 8 scores in the data matrix as in the matrices in Tables 5.1 and 5.2. The SS_{TOTAL} = 17.5 in Table 5.3 as it did in the other two matrices. However, the total sum of squares is partitioned in a third way in Table 5.3. There, the interaction between factors A and B accounts for most of the total variability. By contrast, the interaction between S' and A in the Within-Subjects design (Table 5.2) accounted for very little of the total variability. Finally, it should be clear that the nonsignificant results (i.e., p>.05) in all but the Within-Subjects design is due to the fact that very large F values are required when the df in the numerator and denominator are small.

Table 5.3

Analysis of Data for an $S_2'(A_2)B_2$ Mixed Design

Preliminary Summary Table

SV	df	Expanded df	SS Computational Formulas
A	a-1	a-1	$\overset{a}{\Sigma}(\overset{bs}{\Sigma\Sigma}X)^2/bs - (\overset{abs}{\Sigma\Sigma\Sigma}X)/abs$
B	b-1	b-1	$\overset{b}{\Sigma}(\overset{as}{\Sigma\Sigma}X)^2/as - (\overset{abs}{\Sigma\Sigma\Sigma}X)^2/abs$
AB	(a-1) (b-1)	ab-a-b+1	$\overset{ab}{\Sigma\Sigma}(\overset{s}{\Sigma}X)^2/s - \overset{a}{\Sigma}(\overset{bs}{\Sigma\Sigma}X)^2/bs -$ $\overset{b}{\Sigma}(\overset{as}{\Sigma\Sigma}X)^2/as + (\overset{abs}{\Sigma\Sigma\Sigma}X)^2/abs$
S'(A)	(s-1)(a)	as-a	$\overset{as}{\Sigma\Sigma}(\overset{b}{\Sigma}X)^2/b - \overset{a}{\Sigma}(\overset{bs}{\Sigma\Sigma}X)^2/bs$
S'(A)B	(s-1)(a) (b-1)	abs-as -ab+a	$\overset{abs}{\Sigma\Sigma\Sigma}(X)^2 - \overset{as}{\Sigma\Sigma}(\overset{b}{\Sigma}X)^2/b -$ $\overset{ab}{\Sigma\Sigma}(\overset{s}{\Sigma}X)^2/s + \overset{a}{\Sigma}(\overset{bs}{\Sigma\Sigma}X)^2/bs$
Total	(a)(b) (s)-1	abs-1	$\overset{abs}{\Sigma\Sigma\Sigma}(X)^2 - (\overset{abs}{\Sigma\Sigma\Sigma}X)^2/abs$

Hypothetical Data

		b_1	b_2	$\overset{b}{\Sigma}X$
a_1	s_1	1	3	4
	s_2	0	5	5
		$(\overset{s}{\Sigma}X) = 1$	$(\overset{s}{\Sigma}X) = 8$	$(\overset{bs}{\Sigma\Sigma}X) = 9$
a_2	s_3	1	1	2
	s_4	2	1	3
		$(\overset{s}{\Sigma}X) = 3$	$(\overset{s}{\Sigma}X) = 2$	$(\overset{bs}{\Sigma\Sigma}X) = 5$
		$(\overset{as}{\Sigma\Sigma}X) = 4$	$(\overset{as}{\Sigma\Sigma}X) = 10$	$(\overset{abs}{\Sigma\Sigma\Sigma}X) = 14$
		$\overset{as}{\Sigma\Sigma}(X)^2 = 6$	$\overset{as}{\Sigma\Sigma}(X)^2 = 36$	$(\overset{abs}{\Sigma\Sigma\Sigma}X)^2 = 42$

SS Computations

$$SS_A = [(9^2 + 5^2/4] - (14^2/8) = 26.5 - 24.5 = 2.00$$

$$SS_B = [(4^2 + 10^2)/4] - 24.5 = 29 - 24.5 = 4.50$$

$$SS_{AB} = [(1^2 + 8^2 + 3^2 + 2^2)/2] - 26.5 - 29 + 24.5 = 8.00$$

$$SS_{S'(A)} = [(4^2 + 5^2 + 2^2 + 3^2)/2] - 26.5 = 27 - 26.5 = .50$$

$$SS_{S'(A)B} = 42 - 27 - 39 + 26.5 = 2.50$$

$$SS_{TOTAL} = 42 - 24.5 = 17.50$$

Summary Table

SV	df	SS	MS	F	p
A	1	2.00	2.00	8.00	>.05
B	1	4.50	4.50	3.60	>.05
AB	1	8.00	8.00	6.40	>.05
S'(A)	2	.50	.25	–	
S'(A)B	2	2.50	1.25	–	

Note first that the superscript or the product of superscripts <u>inside</u> the parentheses indicates the number of scores that are summed prior to squaring. For example, $\sum (\sum\sum X)^2/bs$ indicates that each total prior to squaring is made up of <u>bs</u> or $(2)(2) = 4$ scores. Second, the superscript or the product of the superscripts <u>outside</u> the parentheses indicate the number of squared values to be summed. For example, $\sum\sum(\sum X)^2/s$ indicates that there are <u>ab</u> or $(2)(2) = 4$ squared totals, i.e., $(1)^2 + (8)^2 + (3)^2 + (2)^2$. Third, when there are no summation signs outside the parentheses, as for $(\sum\sum\sum X)^2$, it indicates that a single term is squared. Finally, the sum of the terms prior to squaring will always equal the total sum of all the scores. In our example the total sum of scores is 14. Consider the term $\sum(\sum\sum X)^2/bs$ which numerically reduces to $(9^2/4) + (5^2/4)$. Note that the sums to be squared add to the total sum, i.e., $9 + 5 = 14$. These generalizations are common to all summing operations in computational formulas and can be used to verify computations.

As designs become large, small summary tables showing the requisite pieces of information are helpful for computing sums of squares. For example, if there were 20 observations in each of the 4 ab cells in Table 5.3, it would be easier to sum the 20 scores in each cell and enter these sums in a smaller 2 X 2 summary table. Then the information in the summary tables can be used to calculate the sums of squares.

GENERATING COMPUTATIONAL FORMULAS FOR SS

Look again at Tables 5.1, 5.2, and 5.3. Examine the relationship between the "expanded df" formulas and the computational formulas. There are as many terms in the computational formulas as there are in the expanded df formulas. Moreover, there is a link between corresponding terms. This link can be used to develop a rule for generating computational formulas. The rule is outlined in four steps below. When the steps are followed, they generate computational formulas for any source of variance generated by the Source Rule.

1. Assuming that the Degrees of Freedom Rule (from Chapter 4) has been used to generate a df formula, expand the formula for the df associated with each source of variance. For example, the df for an AB source are $(a-1)(b-1)$ which expands to $(ab-a-b+1)$. The df for an S'(AB) source are $(s-1)(ab)$ which expands to $(abs-ab)$.

2. Write a set of parentheses for each term in the expansion, separate each set by the same algebraic sign that separates the terms in the expansion, put the square sign outside each set, and an X within each set; e.g.,

$$ab-a-b+1: \quad (\ X\ )^2 - (\ X\ )^2 - (\ X\ )^2 + (\ X\ )^2$$

$$abs-ab: \quad (\ X\ )^2 - (\ X\ )^2$$

3. (a) Write a summation sign <u>outside</u> the parentheses for each experimental design factor mentioned in the expanded df. (b) Write a summation sign <u>inside</u> the parentheses for each design factor not mentioned in the expansion. Always include superscripts to identify the summation signs.

$$\text{ab}-\text{a}-\text{b}+1:\quad \text{(a)}\ \overset{ab}{\Sigma\Sigma}(\,X)^2 - \overset{a}{\Sigma}(\,X)^2 - \overset{b}{\Sigma}(\,X)^2 + (\,X)^2$$

$$\text{(b)}\ \overset{ab}{\Sigma\Sigma}(\overset{s}{\Sigma}X)^2 - \overset{a}{\Sigma}(\overset{bs}{\Sigma\Sigma}X)^2 - \overset{b}{\Sigma}(\overset{as}{\Sigma\Sigma}X)^2 + (\overset{abs}{\Sigma\Sigma\Sigma}X)^2$$

$$\text{abs}-\text{ab}:\quad \text{(a)}\ \overset{abs}{\Sigma\Sigma\Sigma}(X)^2 - \overset{ab}{\Sigma\Sigma}(\,X)^2$$

$$\text{(b)}\ \overset{abs}{\Sigma\Sigma\Sigma}(X)^2 - \overset{ab}{\Sigma\Sigma}(\overset{s}{\Sigma}X)^2$$

4. Divide each term in the formula by the superscript or product of the superscripts inside the parentheses.

Therefore, the computational formula for an AB source in an S'(AB) design is:

$$SS_{AB} = \overset{ab}{\Sigma\Sigma}(\overset{s}{\Sigma}X)^2/s - \overset{a}{\Sigma}(\overset{bs}{\Sigma\Sigma}X)^2/bs - \overset{b}{\Sigma}(\overset{as}{\Sigma\Sigma}X)^2/as +$$
$$(\overset{abs}{\Sigma\Sigma\Sigma}X)^2/abs$$

and the computational formula for an S'(AB) source in an S'(AB) design is

$$SS_{S'(AB)} = \overset{abs}{\Sigma\Sigma\Sigma}(X)^2 - \overset{ab}{\Sigma\Sigma}(\overset{s}{\Sigma}X)^2/s.$$

Although we have listed four basic steps in deriving the computational formulas, with practice the process becomes unified and rapid. Notice that whenever a 1 appears in the expanded df, <u>all</u> summation signs are placed <u>inside</u> parentheses. If a term in the expanded df involves all of the experimental factors, then all summation signs are placed outside parentheses. In this case there is no division operation; e.g., the first term in the S'(AB) source above. These four steps can be condensed into the Sum of Squares Rule.

<u>Sum of Squares Rule</u>: Expand the df formula produced by the Degrees of Freedom Rule, write a set of squared parenthetical terms for each term in the expansion, place a summation sign outside the parentheses for each letter (design factor) in an expanded df and inside the parentheses for each letter not mentioned, and, finally, divide each term by the product of the superscripts inside the parentheses.

The reader should consult Tables 5.1, 5.2, and 5.3 to see how the Sum of Squares Rule was applied.

READING TERMS

Now that you have encountered a maze of summation signs, parentheses, and a few generalizations, you can better "read" and understand the verbal equivalents of the following terms. We will provide only a few, since the reader should now be able to generate many more.

$\overset{a}{\Sigma}(\overset{s}{\Sigma}X)^2/s$:

Sum all the <u>s</u> scores at each level of A, square each sum, sum all of these squares, and then divide the sum of these squares by <u>s</u>. More briefly, get the sum of the squares of the totals at each A level and divide by <u>s</u>.

$(\overset{as}{\Sigma\Sigma}X)^2/as$:

Sum across S and A, square this total, then divide by <u>as</u>. More briefly, square the total of all <u>as</u> scores and divide by <u>as</u>.

$\overset{as}{\Sigma\Sigma}(X)^2$:

Find the numbers that represent the intersection of each AS level, square each such number, then sum all these squares. More briefly, square each score, then add the squares.

$\overset{c}{\Sigma}(\overset{abs}{\Sigma\Sigma\Sigma}X)^2/abs$:

For each level of C find the sum of the scores across all ABS levels, square each such sum, then sum these squares, and finally, divide by <u>abs</u>. More briefly, square the total of all the scores at each C level, sum these squares, then divide by <u>abs</u>.

$\overset{sc}{\Sigma\Sigma}(\overset{ab}{\Sigma\Sigma}X)^2/ab$:

For each combination of S and C find the sum of all the numbers across each combination of A and B, square each of these CS sums, then sum these squares and, finally, divide by <u>ab</u>. More briefly, sum the squares of the totals at each of the CS combinations and divide by <u>ab</u>.

$\overset{cas}{\Sigma\Sigma\Sigma}(\overset{b}{\Sigma}X)^2/b$:

For each unique combination of C and A and S levels find the sum of all numbers across all B levels, square each of these CAS sums, then sum these squares and, finally, divide by the number of levels of B. More briefly, get the sum of the squares of the totals at each of the CAS combinations and divide by <u>b</u>.

MEAN SQUARES

The purpose of computing sums of squares is to provide the numerator portion of mean squares. Recall that in the analysis of variance, a variance estimate is a mean square (MS) and is defined as SS/df. Thus, in order to compute an MS for each source of variance, the SS for each source is divided by the corresponding df. This has been done in the three summary tables presented in this chapter.

EXERCISES

Analyze the data presented in the three matrices below. As in Tables 5.1, 5.2, and 5.3 construct the preliminary summary tables, compute the sums of squares, and write out a final summary table. The only answers we provide for these exercises are as follows: For exercise 5-1, the mean squares are 2.00, 6.25, and .75. For exercise 5-2, they are 2.00, 4.50, 0.00, and 2.75, and for exercise 5-3, they are 2.00, 4.50, 8.00, .50, and 1.00.

Exercise 5-1

		a_1	1 0
	b_1		
		a_2	3 5
		a_3	1 2
	b_2		
		a_4	1 1

Exercise 5-2

	b_1	b_2
a_1	1 0	3 1
a_2	1 2	5 1

Exercise 5-3

	b_1		b_2	
	a_1	a_2	a_3	a_4
s_1	1	0	3	5
s_2	1	2	1	1

6

EXPECTED MEAN SQUARES AND F RATIOS

As discussed in Chapter 2, no amount of experimental control can eliminate variability from a set of data. Fortunately, the analysis of variance allows us to specify the particular contribution various sources make to the overall variability. This is done by forming F ratios that, under the null hypothesis of no treatment effects, contain two independent estimates of the variance attributable to the same source. We call these estimates mean squares (MS).

For any F ratio, the mean square in the numerator contains an estimate of the variance due to the particular factor or combinations of factors of interest, and an estimate of the variance due to some other components as well. These latter components are usually referred to collectively as error variance. If the null hypothesis is true and there are no treatment effects, no effects of the factor of interest, then the numerator mean square only estimates the error variance. When the null hypothesis is false, and some treatment effects do exist, the value of the numerator reflects them. The mean square in the denominator is an estimate of the numerator's error variance regardless of the truth about the null hypothesis. Because we assume the null hypothesis to be true, the expected value of F is 1, since in this case the F ratio would contain two estimates of the same error variance. If the null hypothesis is false, then the F value will be greater than 1 since in this case we have

$$\underline{F} = \frac{\text{treatment effect + error}}{\text{error}}$$

A critical step in determining the contribution a factor, or combination of factors, makes to the dependent measure, is to identify the appropriate denominator. For each $\underline{F}$ test a denominator is needed that contains only components that are considered error variance in the numerator. This problem reduces to determining precisely which variance components contribute to each mean square, since an appropriate $\underline{F}$ ratio cannot be formed without knowing which sources of variance contribute to the numerator's error variance. In other words, we need to know which sources of variance can be expected to influence the value of the numerator mean square. These expected values of the mean square are called expected mean squares (EMS).

Many researchers consider the problem of generating expected mean squares to be formidable. In fact, this problem is often considered the toughest nut to crack in an analysis of variance procedure. It turns out, however, that a simple rule, the Expected Mean Square Rule, can be used to generate expected mean squares quickly and efficiently.

DETERMINATION OF EXPECTED MEAN SQUARES

The expected mean square for a source of variance can be determined quite easily. Aside from the source of variance itself, fixed factors do not contribute to EMSs because their effects are assumed to be constant, and the variance is not changed by adding or subtracting a constant from the raw scores that enter into the variance. However, the effects of a random factor are, by definition, not constant, and therefore they do affect the variance. Keep in mind here that an $\underline{F}$ ratio is a ratio of two variances. We have already seen that the numerator and denominator contain a variable error component, but the numerator most often contains a fixed effect component as well since treatment factors are usually fixed. Random effects can contribute to the numerator or denominator of an $\underline{F}$ ratio, but fixed effects do not contribute to the denominator since adding or subtracting a constant from the scores of subjects in a group does not change the within-group variance. This variance serves as the error term for evaluating between-group or treatment effects. In general, the denominator mean square represents the contribution of random factors to the variability in the scores. For this reason, this mean square is often called the error mean square or, simply, the error term. The EMS Rule encapsulizes the above considerations.

Expected Mean Square Rule: A source of variance X contributes to the expected mean square for source of variance Y if: (a) X contains Y, and (b) X contains only random factors (besides Y) outside of its outermost parentheses.

It is rather easy, using the General Notation System, to illustrate the EMS Rule. For example, suppose we wish to obtain the EMS for some source of variance A. The following sources of variance, if present in a design with A, would contribute to its EMS:

S'(A), S'(AB), AB', AB'C', A(B)C', B'(C(A))

Clearly each of these variance components (the "X's" in the EMS Rule) contains A. And, when a component contains parentheses (i.e., when nesting is present), all factors outside the outermost parentheses must be random in order for that component to contribute. If even one of these factors is fixed, except A itself, then the component does not contribute to the EMS for A. Given these considerations, the following variance components would not contribute to the EMS for A:

BC, S'(A)B, AB, ABC', A(B)C, B(C(A))

In a design with an A'(B) source, the following sources of variance would contribute to the EMS for A'(B):

S'(A'(B)), A'(B)C', S'(C(A'(B))), S'A'(B),

whereas

C'(D)E', A'(B)C, C(A'(B)), S'B, and B

would not.

In conclusion, the EMS for a particular source of variance can be determined by following the EMS Rule.

This process can be conceptualized as the series of questions diagrammed in Figure 6.1.

Figure 6.1

A Picture of the EMS Rule

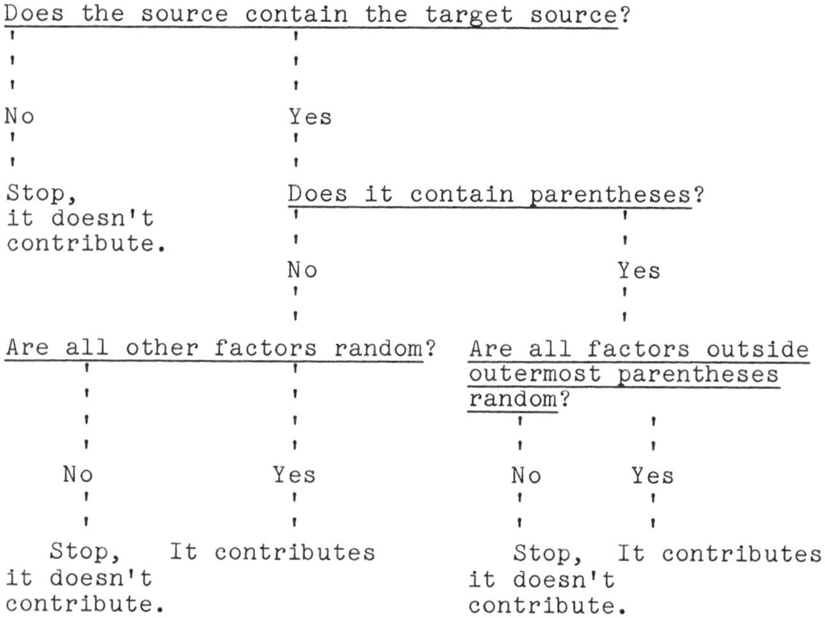

Does the source contain the target source?
```
 ┊               ┊
 ┊               ┊
 ┊               ┊
No              Yes
 ┊               ┊
 ┊               ┊
Stop,           Does it contain parentheses?
it doesn't       ┊                         ┊
contribute.      ┊                         ┊
                No                        Yes
                 ┊                         ┊
                 ┊                         ┊
Are all other factors random?   Are all factors outside
 ┊               ┊               outermost parentheses
 ┊               ┊               random?
 ┊               ┊                ┊               ┊
 ┊               ┊                ┊               ┊
No              Yes              No              Yes
 ┊               ┊                ┊               ┊
 ┊               ┊                ┊               ┊
    Stop,    It contributes          Stop,    It contributes
it doesn't                       it doesn't
contribute.                      contribute.
```

The first question is whether a source of variance, i.e., X, contains the source in question. If it does not, then X doesn't contribute. If it does, then ask the second question: Does it contain parentheses? If not, then ask whether all of its factors are random. If all the factors are random, then X contributes. If any factors are not random, then X does not contribute. If the source does contain parentheses, ask whether all factors outside the outermost parentheses are random. If all such factors are random, then X contributes. If any of the factors outside the parentheses are not random, then X does not contribute.

Thus far EMSs have been presented in a somewhat simplified form. The EMS Rule accomplishes what most investigators wish, but it sidesteps the mathematical complexities of expected values (see Ferguson, 1971, or Winer, 1962, for a more complete discussion of EMSs). It is possible, however, to write the EMSs in terms of variance components as Table 6.1 illustrates for an $S_{10}'(A_2)B_2$ mixed design. Note that each contributing variance component is weighted by the product of the subscripts of the factors not indicated in the source but nevertheless present in the experimental design (see the fourth column in Table 6.1). For simplicity, we will continue to use the first method introduced, as shown in the second column in Table 6.1.

Table 6.1

EMS and F Ratios for an $S_{10}'(A_2)B_2$ Design

SV	EMS	EMS in General	EMS Values	F Ratios
A	A + S'(A)	$sb\sigma_A^2 + b\sigma_{S'(A)}^2$	$20\sigma_A^2 + 2\sigma_{S'(A)}^2$	$MS_A/MS_{S'(A)}$
B	B + S'(A)B	$sa\sigma_B^2 + \sigma_{S'(A)B}^2$	$20\sigma_B^2 + \sigma_{S'(A)B}^2$	$MS_B/MS_{S'(A)B}$
S'(A)	S'(A)	$b\sigma_{S'(A)}^2$	$2\sigma_{S'(A)}^2$	−
AB	AB + S'(A)B	$s\sigma_{AB}^2 + \sigma_{S'(A)B}^2$	$10\sigma_{AB}^2 + \sigma_{S'(A)B}^2$	$MS_{AB}/MS_{S'(A)B}$
S'(A)B	S'(A)B	$\sigma_{S'(A)B}^2$	$\sigma_{S'(A)B}^2$	−

SELECTION OF ERROR TERMS

Once the EMSs have been generated for all of the sources of variance in an experimental design, the selection of error term mean squares becomes a relatively simple matter. For each source of variance one attempts to find another source of variance whose EMS contains all but one of the variance components in the source of interest. The missing component corresponds to the effect whose significance is being evaluated. For example, if a source A has as its EMS

91

the components A, X, and Y, and a source X has as its components X and Y, then the MS for X can be used as the error term to evaluate A. We can elevate this simple idea to the status of a rule called the Error Term Rule.

> Error Term Rule: To select an error term for an effect, use a source of variance whose EMS contains all the variance components in the EMS for the effect, except the component that corresponds to the effect itself.

Appropriate error terms are usually either easy or impossible to find. Examination of Table 6.1 shows, for example, that S'(A) is the appropriate error term for the A effect, since the EMS for A is A + S'(A) while that for S'(A) is S'(A). Thus, the

$$\underline{F} \text{ test for A effect} = \frac{A + S'(A)}{S'(A)}$$

which obviously has an expected value of 1 if the null hypothesis -- that A has no effect -- is true. If it is not true, then the expected value of $\underline{F}$ is greater than 1. Similar logic applies to the B effect where the appropriate

$$\underline{F} \text{ test for B effect} = \frac{B + S'(A)B}{S'(A)B}$$

Thus B is evaluated by placing the mean square for B over the mean square for S'(A)B to form an F ratio. Finally, the required

$$\underline{F} \text{ test for AB effect} = \frac{AB + S'(A)B}{S'(A)B}$$

Thus, the AB effect is evaluated by dividing the AB mean square by the S'(A)B mean square.

The statistical significance of the A, B, and AB effects is determined by consulting an $\underline{F}$ table as described in Chapter 2. Recall that this is done by finding the $\underline{F}$ value in the table defined by the a priori Alpha value, and the numerator and denominator df. If the obtained $\underline{F}$ value equals or exceeds this tabled value, then the $\overline{\underline{F}}$ is said to be **significant,** and the null hypothesis is rejected. This conclusion implies, of course, that the effect in question is a real (non-chance) effect. If the obtained $\underline{F}$ value is less than the required tabled value, then the $\overline{\underline{F}}$ is said to be non-significant and the null hypothesis is not rejected as an erroneous hypothesis. This result implies that the effect in question can be considered to have arisen by chance.

We have yet to consider the sources of variance in Table 6.1 that contain the S' factor. Clearly, neither the S'(A) nor the S'(A)B sources can be evaluated since an appropriate denominator EMS cannot be found for them. This is the typical state of affairs in experimental designs: Mean squares involving S' effects regularly serve as error terms for treatment factors but cannot be evaluated themselves. Even in fixed factor within-subject designs, in which S' can be isolated as a source of variance, it usually cannot be evaluated for significance since appropriate error terms do not exist. It is only when a treatment factor is random that the S' factor can possibly be evaluated. For example, in an S'A' design the S' effect can be evaluated since an appropriate ratio exists in the following form:

$$\underline{F} \text{ ratio for S' effect in an S'A' design} = \frac{S'+S'A'}{S'A'}$$

Still, most investigators are not interested in effects involving the subject factor, even when they can be evaluated, since a significant S' effect indicates only that subjects are different -- something quite well known.

A more difficult problem crops up when an investigator wishes to evaluate certain treatment effects, but no single appropriate denominator EMS can be found. This inevitably happens in designs that have one or more random treatment factors. For example, consider an S'AB' design, even though this sort of design is unlikely. The sources of variance, EMSs and $\underline{F}$ ratios for an S'AB' design are given in Table 6.2.

Table 6.2

EMSs and $\underline{F}$ Ratios for an S'AB' Design

SV	EMS	F Ratios
S'	S' + S'B'	$MS_{S'}/MS_{S'B'}$
A*	A + S'A + AB' + S'AB'	$MS_A/MS_{S'A}+MS_{AB'}-MS_{S'AB'}$
B'	B' + S'B'	$MS_B/MS_{S'B'}$
S'A	S'A + S'AB'	$MS_{S'A}/MS_{S'AB'}$
S'B'	S'B'	—
AB'	AB' + S'AB'	$MS_{AB}/MS_{S'AB'}$
S'AB'	S'AB'	—

*Note the EMS and $\underline{F}$ ratio for this source.

Notice that there is no single source of variance term that can serve as an appropriate denominator for the A effect. Should we "give up" then, and leave it at that? Not necessarily. Some statisticians suggest that a quasi-F ratio might be used where two or more EMSs are combined linearly to obtain the required error term. Note that in Table 6.2 the error term for the A source is composed of three mean squares. This is an appropriate error term since adding the EMSs for the S'A and AB' sources and subtracting the EMS for the S'AB' source yields S'A + AB' + S'AB', the error variance in the numerator. That is:

$$EMS_{S'A} + EMS_{AB'} - EMS_{S'AB'}$$

$$= (S'A + S'AB') + (AB' + S'AB') - (S'AB')$$

$$= S'A + AB' + S'AB'$$

In discussing quasi-$\underline{F}$ ratios, Myers (1979, pp. 190-192) notes that another quasi-$\underline{F}$ ratio is possible as a test of the A effect in the above design:

$$\text{F test for the A effect} = \frac{MS_A + MS_{S'AB'}}{MS_{AB'} + MS_{S'A}}$$

Unfortunately, it is not clear which quasi-$\underline{F}$ ratio should be used for the example at hand, but Myers seems to prefer the first mentioned. For further information generally, and to determine the appropriate df for the quasi-$\underline{F}$ ratios, we suggest that the reader consult Myers' discussion.

One last critical point needs to be made here. Recall from Chapter 2 that the analysis of variance procedure assumes that each score can be modeled as the sum of several variance components. Recall also that the particular components included in the model are dictated by the researcher's theory. Therefore, the variance components that appear in the EMS for particular sources depend totally on the score model for the experiment. For example, experimenters sometimes (though quite infrequently!) assume that interaction effects are negligible and therefore omit these effects from the score model. In this case, the experimenter also assumes that none of the overall variance is attributable to the interaction of treatment effects. The practical effect of this assumption is that interaction sources of variance are not entered as sources of variance in the summary table and cannot become components in EMSs. This tends to simplify matters, but it is usually not very realistic from a behavioral standpoint since interactions between variables are commonplace in behavioral research. Our strategy in using the EMS Rule is to assume that if an effect can be isolated as a source of variance, it should be entered in a summary table and appear in the appropriate EMSs.

Thus, if it is assumed in an S'A design that the S'A interaction is not present in the score model, then the S' factor can be evaluated. Since, as mentioned above, this is generally a poor assumption, one is better advised to include the S'A effect in the score model, in which case the S' effect cannot be evaluated since no appropriate EMS exists. As in the first or non-interaction case, the A effect can be evaluated, but it should be clear that the

$$EMS_A = \text{Error} + A + S'A$$

and the

$$EMS_{S'A} = Error + S'A$$

That is, the error term is composed of the S'A inter-action component in addition to an error component. Theoretically, an error component is present in all experiments. In Between-Subject or Mixed designs, this component is estimated by sources such as S'(A), S'(AB), etc., that act as error terms. In other words, the mean square for S'(A) is the error in an S'(A) design, S'(AB) is the error in an S'(AB) design, and so on. Lee (1975, pp. 82-83) states that error terms for "single measurement" designs contain two components, one which is systematic and will not vary if a subject is measured under the same treatment, and one which is variable and will vary randomly for each measurement. According to Lee, these two components are confounded (inextricably mixed) in single measurement designs and cannot be isolated. In repeated measurements designs, however, they can be isolated.

EXERCISES

Derive the EMSs and F ratios for the designs notated in the exercises for Chapter 1. The answers for the even numbered problems are given in Appendix B.

REFERENCES

Dixon, W.J. (Ed.). BMDP. Biomedical computer programs. P-series. Berkeley, California: University of California Press, 1981.

Edwards, A.L. Experimental design in psychological research (4th ed.). New York: Holt, Rinehart and Winston, Inc., 1972.

Ferguson, G.A. Statistical analysis in psychology & education (3rd ed.). New York: McGraw-Hill Co., 1971.

Gaito, J. Introduction to analysis of variance procedures. New York: MSS Information Corporation, 1973.

Hays, W.L. Statistics for psychologists. New York: Holt, Rinehart and Winston, 1963.

Helwig, J.T., & Council, K.A. (Eds.). SAS user's guide. 1979 Edition. Cary, North Carolina: SAS Institute Inc., 1979.

Hull, C.H., & Nie, N.H. SPSS update: New procedures and facilities for releases 7 and 8. New York: McGraw-Hill Book Co., 1979.

Keppel, G. Design and analysis: A researcher's handbook. Englewood Cliffs, New Jersey: Prentice-Hall, Inc., 1973.

Kirk, R.E. Experimental design: Procedures for the behavioral sciences. Monterey, Calif.: Brooks/Cole, 1968.

Lee, W. Experimental design and analysis. San Francisco: W.H. Freeman and Company, 1975.

McNemar, Q. Psychological statistics (3rd ed.). New York: John Wiley and Sons, Inc., 1962.

Millman, J., & Glass, G.V. Rules of thumb for writing the anova table. Journal of Educational Measurement, 1967, 4, 41-51.

Myers, J.L. Fundamentals of experimental design (3rd ed.). Boston: Allyn and Bacon, Inc., 1979.

Nie, N.H., Hull, C.H., Jenkins, J.G., Steinbrenner, K., & Bent, D.H. SPSS: Statistical package for the social sciences (2nd ed.). New York: McGraw-Hill Book Co., 1975.

Winer, B.J. Statistical principles in experimental design. New York: McGraw-Hill, 1962.

Table of F for .05 (roman), .01 (*italic*), and .001 (bold face)
levels of significance*

n_2 \ n_1	1	2	3	4	5	6	8	12	24	∞
1	161	200	216	225	230	234	239	244	249	254
	4052	*4999*	*5403*	*5625*	*5724*	*5859*	*5981*	*6106*	*6234*	*6366*
	405284	**500000**	**540379**	**562500**	**576405**	**585937**	**598144**	**610667**	**623497**	**636619**
2	18.51	19.00	19.16	19.25	19.30	19.33	19.37	19.41	19.45	19.50
	98.49	*99.01*	*99.17*	*99.25*	*99.30*	*99.33*	*99.36*	*99.42*	*99.46*	*99.50*
	998.5	**999.0**	**999.2**	**999.2**	**999.3**	**999.3**	**999.4**	**999.4**	**999.5**	**999.5**
3	10.13	9.55	9.28	9.12	9.01	8.94	8.84	8.74	8.64	8.53
	34.12	*30.81*	*29.46*	*28.71*	*28.24*	*27.91*	*27.49*	*27.05*	*26.60*	*26.12*
	167.5	**148.5**	**141.1**	**137.1**	**134.6**	**132.8**	**130.6**	**128.3**	**125.9**	**123.5**
4	7.71	6.94	6.59	6.39	6.26	6.16	6.04	5.91	5.77	5.63
	21.20	*18.00*	*16.69*	*15.98*	*15.52*	*15.21*	*14.80*	*14.37*	*13.93*	*13.46*
	74.14	**61.25**	**56.18**	**53.44**	**51.71**	**50.53**	**49.00**	**47.41**	**45.77**	**44.05**
5	6.61	5.79	5.41	5.19	5.05	4.95	4.82	4.68	4.53	4.36
	16.26	*13.27*	*12.06*	*11.39*	*10.97*	*10.67*	*10.27*	*9.89*	*9.47*	*9.02*
	47.04	**36.61**	**33.20**	**31.09**	**29.75**	**28.84**	**27.64**	**26.42**	**25.14**	**23.78**
6	5.99	5.14	4.76	4.53	4.39	4.28	4.15	4.00	3.84	3.67
	13.74	*10.92*	*9.78*	*9.15*	*8.75*	*8.47*	*8.10*	*7.72*	*7.31*	*6.88*
	35.51	**27.00**	**23.70**	**21.90**	**20.81**	**20.03**	**19.03**	**17.99**	**16.89**	**15.75**
7	5.59	4.74	4.35	4.12	3.97	3.87	3.73	3.57	3.41	3.23
	12.25	*9.55*	*8.45*	*7.85*	*7.46*	*7.19*	*6.84*	*6.47*	*6.07*	*5.65*
	29.22	**21.69**	**18.77**	**17.19**	**16.21**	**15.52**	**14.63**	**13.71**	**12.73**	**11.69**
8	5.32	4.46	4.07	3.84	3.69	3.58	3.44	3.28	3.12	2.93
	11.26	*8.65*	*7.59*	*7.01*	*6.63*	*6.37*	*6.03*	*5.67*	*5.28*	*4.86*
	25.42	**18.49**	**15.83**	**14.39**	**13.49**	**12.86**	**12.04**	**11.19**	**10.30**	**9.34**
9	5.12	4.26	3.86	3.63	3.48	3.37	3.23	3.07	2.90	2.71
	10.56	*8.02*	*6.99*	*6.42*	*6.06*	*5.80*	*5.47*	*5.11*	*4.73*	*4.31*
	22.86	**16.39**	**13.90**	**12.56**	**11.71**	**11.13**	**10.37**	**9.57**	**8.72**	**7.81**
10	4.96	4.10	3.71	3.48	3.33	3.22	3.07	2.91	2.74	2.54
	10.04	*7.56*	*6.55*	*5.99*	*5.64*	*5.39*	*5.06*	*4.71*	*4.33*	*3.91*
	21.04	**14.91**	**12.55**	**11.28**	**10.48**	**9.92**	**9.20**	**8.45**	**7.64**	**6.76**
11	4.84	3.98	3.59	3.36	3.20	3.09	2.95	2.79	2.61	2.40
	9.65	*7.20*	*6.22*	*5.67*	*5.32*	*5.07*	*4.74*	*4.40*	*4.02*	*3.60*
	19.69	**13.81**	**11.56**	**10.35**	**9.58**	**9.05**	**8.35**	**7.63**	**6.85**	**6.00**
12	4.75	3.88	3.49	3.26	3.11	3.00	2.85	2.69	2.50	2.30
	9.33	*6.93*	*5.95*	*5.41*	*5.06*	*4.82*	*4.50*	*4.16*	*3.78*	*3.36*
	18.64	**12.97**	**10.80**	**9.63**	**8.89**	**8.38**	**7.71**	**7.00**	**6.25**	**5.42**

Table of F for .05 (roman), .01 (*italic*), and .001 (bold face) levels of significance* (*continued*)

n_2 \ n_1	1	2	3	4	5	6	8	12	24	∞
13	4.67	3.80	3.41	3.18	3.02	2.92	2.77	2.60	2.42	2.21
	9.07	6.70	5.74	5.20	4.86	4.62	4.30	3.96	3.59	3.16
	17.81	**12.31**	**10.21**	**9.07**	**8.35**	**7.86**	**7.21**	**6.52**	**5.78**	**4.97**
14	4.60	3.74	3.34	3.11	2.96	2.85	2.70	2.53	2.35	2.13
	8.86	6.51	5.56	5.03	4.69	4.46	4.14	3.80	3.43	3.00
	17.14	**11.78**	**9.73**	**8.62**	**7.92**	**7.43**	**6.80**	**6.13**	**5.41**	**4.60**
15	4.54	3.68	3.29	3.06	2.90	2.79	2.64	2.48	2.29	2.07
	8.68	6.36	5.42	4.89	4.56	4.32	4.00	3.67	3.29	2.87
	16.59	**11.34**	**9.34**	**8.25**	**7.57**	**7.09**	**6.47**	**5.81**	**5.10**	**4.31**
16	4.49	3.63	3.24	3.01	2.85	2.74	2.59	2.42	2.24	2.01
	8.53	6.23	5.29	4.77	4.44	4.20	3.89	3.55	3.18	2.75
	16.12	**10.97**	**9.00**	**7.94**	**7.27**	**6.81**	**6.19**	**5.55**	**4.85**	**4.06**
17	4.45	3.59	3.20	2.96	2.81	2.70	2.55	2.38	2.19	1.96
	8.40	6.11	5.18	4.67	4.34	4.10	3.79	3.45	3.08	2.65
	15.72	**10.66**	**8.73**	**7.68**	**7.02**	**6.56**	**5.96**	**5.32**	**4.63**	**3.85**
18	4.41	3.55	3.16	2.93	2.77	2.66	2.51	2.34	2.15	1.92
	8.28	6.01	5.09	4.58	4.25	4.01	3.71	3.37	3.00	2.57
	15.38	**10.39**	**8.49**	**7.46**	**6.81**	**6.35**	**5.76**	**5.13**	**4.45**	**3.67**
19	4.38	3.52	3.13	2.90	2.74	2.63	2.48	2.31	2.11	1.88
	8.18	5.93	5.01	4.50	4.17	3.94	3.63	3.30	2.92	2.49
	15.08	**10.16**	**8.28**	**7.26**	**6.61**	**6.18**	**5.59**	**4.97**	**4.29**	**3.52**
20	4.35	3.49	3.10	2.87	2.71	2.60	2.45	2.28	2.08	1.84
	8.10	5.85	4.94	4.43	4.10	3.87	3.56	3.23	2.86	2.42
	14.82	**9.95**	**8.10**	**7.10**	**6.46**	**6.02**	**5.44**	**4.82**	**4.15**	**3.38**
21	4.32	3.47	3.07	2.84	2.68	2.57	2.42	2.25	2.05	1.81
	8.02	5.78	4.87	4.37	4.04	3.81	3.51	3.17	2.80	2.36
	14.59	**9.77**	**7.94**	**6.95**	**6.32**	**5.88**	**5.31**	**4.70**	**4.03**	**3.26**
22	4.30	3.44	3.05	2.82	2.66	2.55	2.40	2.23	2.03	1.78
	7.94	5.72	4.82	4.31	3.99	3.76	3.45	3.12	2.75	2.31
	14.38	**9.61**	**7.80**	**6.81**	**6.19**	**5.76**	**5.19**	**4.58**	**3.92**	**3.15**
23	4.28	3.42	3.03	2.80	2.64	2.53	2.38	2.20	2.00	1.76
	7.88	5.66	4.76	4.26	3.94	3.71	3.41	3.07	2.70	2.26
	14.19	**9.47**	**7.67**	**6.69**	**6.08**	**5.65**	**5.09**	**4.48**	**3.82**	**3.05**
24	4.26	3.40	3.01	2.78	2.62	2.51	2.36	2.18	1.98	1.73
	7.82	5.61	4.72	4.22	3.90	3.67	3.36	3.03	2.66	2.21
	14.03	**9.34**	**7.55**	**6.59**	**5.98**	**5.55**	**4.99**	**4.39**	**3.74**	**2.97**

**Table of *F* for .05 (roman), .01 (*italic*), and .001 (bold face)
levels of significance*** (*continued*)

n_2 \ n_1	1	2	3	4	5	6	8	12	24	∞
25	4.24	3.38	2.99	2.76	2.60	2.49	2.34	2.16	1.96	1.71
	7.77	*5.57*	*4.68*	*4.18*	*3.86*	*3.63*	*3.32*	*2.99*	*2.62*	*2.17*
	13.88	**9.22**	**7.45**	**6.49**	**5.88**	**5.46**	**4.91**	**4.31**	**3.66**	**2.89**
26	4.22	3.37	2.98	2.74	2.59	2.47	2.32	2.15	1.95	1.69
	7.22	*5.53*	*4.64*	*4.14*	*3.82*	*3.59*	*3.29*	*2.96*	*2.58*	*2.13*
	13.74	**9.12**	**7.36**	**6.41**	**5.80**	**5.38**	**4.83**	**4.24**	**3.59**	**2.82**
27	4.21	3.35	2.96	2.73	2.57	2.46	2.30	2.13	1.93	1.67
	7.68	*5.49*	*4.60*	*4.11*	*3.78*	*3.56*	*3.26*	*2.93*	*2.55*	*2.10*
	13.61	**9.02**	**7.27**	**6.33**	**5.73**	**5.31**	**4.76**	**4.17**	**3.52**	**2.75**
28	4.20	3.34	2.95	2.71	2.56	2.44	2.29	2.12	1.91	1.65
	7.64	*5.45*	*4.57*	*4.07*	*3.75*	*3.53*	*3.23*	*2.90*	*2.52*	*2.06*
	13.50	**8.93**	**7.19**	**6.25**	**5.66**	**5.24**	**4.69**	**4.11**	**3.46**	**2.70**
29	4.18	3.33	2.93	2.70	2.54	2.43	2.28	2.10	1.90	1.64
	7.60	*5.42*	*4.54*	*4.04*	*3.73*	*3.50*	*3.20*	*2.87*	*2.49*	*2.03*
	13.39	**8.85**	**7.12**	**6.19**	**5.59**	**5.18**	**4.64**	**4.05**	**3.41**	**2.64**
30	4.17	3.32	2.92	2.69	2.53	2.42	2.27	2.09	1.89	1.62
	7.56	*5.39*	*4.51*	*4.02*	*3.70*	*3.47*	*3.17*	*2.84*	*2.47*	*2.01*
	13.29	**8.77**	**7.05**	**6.12**	**5.53**	**5.12**	**4.58**	**4.00**	**3.36**	**2.59**
40	4.08	3.23	2.84	2.61	2.45	2.34	2.18	2.00	1.79	1.51
	7.31	*5.18*	*4.31*	*3.83*	*3.51*	*3.29*	*2.99*	*2.66*	*2.29*	*1.80*
	12.61	**8.25**	**6.60**	**5.70**	**5.13**	**4.73**	**4.21**	**3.64**	**3.01**	**2.23**
60	4.00	3.15	2.76	2.52	2.37	2.25	2.10	1.92	1.70	1.39
	7.08	*4.98*	*4.13*	*3.65*	*3.34*	*3.12*	*2.82*	*2.50*	*2.12*	*1.60*
	11.97	**7.76**	**6.17**	**5.31**	**4.76**	**4.37**	**3.87**	**3.31**	**2.69**	**1.90**
120	3.92	3.07	2.68	2.45	2.29	2.17	2.02	1.83	1.61	1.25
	6.85	*4.79*	*3.95*	*3.48*	*3.17*	*2.96*	*2.66*	*2.34*	*1.95*	*1.38*
	11.38	**7.31**	**5.79**	**4.95**	**4.42**	**4.04**	**3.55**	**3.02**	**2.40**	**1.56**
∞	3.84	2.99	2.60	2.37	2.21	2.09	1.94	1.75	1.52	1.00
	6.64	*4.60*	*3.78*	*3.32*	*3.02*	*2.80*	*2.51*	*2.18*	*1.79*	*1.00*
	10.83	**6.91**	**5.42**	**4.62**	**4.10**	**3.74**	**3.27**	**2.74**	**2.13**	**1.00**

*Appendix A is taken, in rearranged form, from Table V of Fisher & Yates: Statistical Tables for Biological, Agricultural and Medical Research, published by Longman Group Ltd., London (previously published by Oliver and Boyd Ltd., Edinburgh) and by permission of the authors and publishers. The Appendix is reproduced from McNemar (1962).

APPENDIX B   Answers To Exercises

Chapter 1

2. $S_5'(A_2B_3C_2)$

	a_1			a_2		
	b_1	b_2	b_3	b_1	b_2	b_3
	c_1 c_2	c_1 c_2	c_1 c_2	c_1 c_2	c_1 c_2	c_1 c_2

s_1 s_6 s_{26} s_{31} s_{56}
. .   . .
. .   . .
s_5 s_{10} s_{30} s_{35} s_{60}

N = 60, no pseudofactors, total number of observations = 60

4. $S_{10}'A_3$

	a_1	a_2	a_3

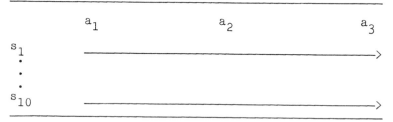

s_1
.
.
.
s_{10}

N = 10, no pseudofactors, total number of observations = 30

6. $S_7'A_2'(B_3)$

	b_1		b_2		b_3	
	a_1	a_2	a_3	a_4	a_5	a_6
s_1	————————————————————>					
$\cdot$						
$\cdot$						
s_7	————————————————————>					

N = 7, A' is pseudofactor with 6 levels, total
number of observations = 42

8. $S_3'(A_3B_2)C_2$

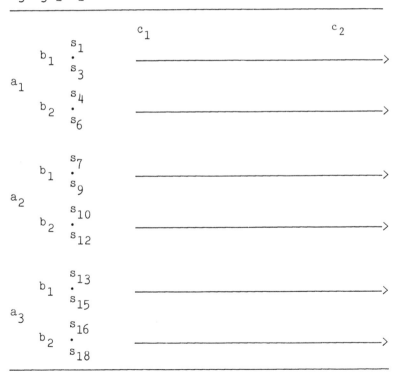

N = 18, no pseudofactors, number of observations = 36

10. $S_5'[U_2'(B_2)]T_2'(A_3)$

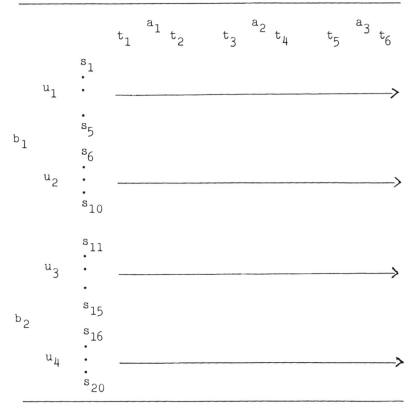

N = 20, U' is a pseudofactor with 4 levels and T' is a pseudofactor with 6 levels, total number of observations = 120

Chapters 3, 4, and 6

2. $S_5'(A_2B_3C_2)$

SV*	df	EMS	F Ratio
1. A	1	1+8	1/8
2. B	2	2+8	2/8
3. C	1	3+8	3/8
4. AB	2	4+8	4/8
5. AC	1	5+8	5/8
6. BC	2	6+8	6/8
7. ABC	2	7+8	7/8
8. S'(ABC)	48	8	–

*Note that we have numbered the SV and have used the numbers in generating EMSs and $\underline{F}$ ratios. This also applies to problems 4, 6, 8, and 10 below.

4. $S_{10}'A_3$

SV	df	EMS	F Ratio
1. S'	9	1	–
2. A	2	2+3	2/3
3. S'A	18	3	–

6. $S_7'A_2'(B_3)$

SV	df	EMS	F Rati
1. S'	6	1+5	1/5
2. B	2	2+3+4+5	*2/3·'
3. S'B	12	3+5	3/⁵
4. A'(B)	3	4+5	4/
5. S'A'(B)	18	5	–

*This is a quasi-$\underline{F}$ ratio or $\underline{F}'$.

105

8. $S_3'(A_3B_2)C_2$

	SV	df	EMS	F Ratio
1.	A	2	1+7	1/7
2.	B	1	2+7	2/7
3.	C	1	3+9	3/9
4.	AB	2	4+7	4/7
5.	AC	2	5+9	5/9
6.	BC	1	6+9	6/9
7.	S'(AB)	12	7	–
8.	ABC	2	8+9	8/9
9.	S'(AB)C	12	9	–

10. $S_5'[U_2'(B_2)]T_2'(A_3)$

	SV	df	EMS	F Ratio
1.	B	1	1+3+6+8+10+11	*1/3+8-10
2.	A	2	2+5+7+9+10+11	*2/5+7-10
3.	U'(B)	2	3+6+10+11	*3/6+10-11
4.	BA	2	4+7+8+9+10+11	*4/7+8-10
5.	T'(A)	3	5+10+11	5/10
6.	S'[U'(B)]	16	6+11	6/11
7.	U'(B)A	4	7+9+10+11	*7/9+10-11
8.	BT'(A)	3	8+10+11	8/10
9.	S'[U'(B)]A	32	9+11	9/11
10.	U'(B)T'(A)	6	10+11	10/11
11.	S'[U'(B)]T'(A)	48	11	–

*This is a quasi-F ratio.

SUBJECT AND AUTHOR INDEX

A

Alpha level, 47, <u>see also</u> Significance level
Analysis of variance, 39-52

B

Between design, 24, <u>see</u> Design, Between-Subjects

C

Completely randomized design, 13, <u>see also</u> Nesting
Computational formulas for SS, 72-75
   Reading of, 83-84
Council, K.A., 4
Critical F value, 46
Crossing
   And nesting in designs, 18-23
   Compared with nesting, 12
   Complete crossing, 11
   Designs involving, 15-18
   Partial crossing, 11

D

Degrees of freedom (df), 45, 61-70
   In Between-Subjects designs, 65
   In Mixed designs, 66
   In Within-Subjects designs, 62
   Methods for obtaining, 63-65
   Table of in several designs, 69

Ferguson, G.A., 91
Fixed effects model, 51
Fixed factors, 10

G

Gaito, J., 48
General Notation System (GNS)
    And experimental design, 6-38
    Computer applications, 4-5
    How to read the GNS, 28-29
    In general, 2-3
    Restrictions on, 12
Generalizability, 8
Glass, G.V., 4
Grand mean, 39

H

Hays, W.L., 10
Hierarchical designs, 14
Helwig, J.T., 4
Honeck, R.P., 5
Hull, C.H., 5
Hypotheses
    Research, 41
        Alternative, 42
        Null, 42
    Statistical, 42
        Alternative, 42
        Null, 42

I

Independent variable, 39, see also
    Experimental treatment factor
Interaction, 17, 50, 78

K

Keppel, G., 3, 4, 47, 48
Kirk, R.E., 3

L

Lee, W., 3, 4, 96
Levels, 9

M

Mean Square (MS), 45, 87
  As error, 89
  Defined, 84-85
  Expected, 87-96
  In analysis of variance, 45
Millman, J., 4
Myers, J.L., 3, 4, 15, 63, 65, 94, 95

N

Nested factor, 11
Nesting
  And crossing in designs, 18-23
  Complete nesting, 11
  Designs involving, 12-14
  Factor, 11
  Partial nesting, 11
  Ultimate nesting factor, 14
Nie, N.H., 4, 5

O

Orthogonal, 12, see also Crossing, and Factorial

Treatment, 40, <u>see also</u> Experimental treatment factor
  Effect, 44
  Population, 41

    U

Ultimate nesting factor, 14
Unbiased estimate, 45, 61

    W

Winer, B.J., 3, 91
Within designs, 24, <u>see</u> Design, Within-Subjects

ABOUT THE AUTHORS

Richard P. Honeck obtained his Ph.D. in experimental psychology in 1969 at the University of Wisconsin-Madison. Clare T. Kibler earned her M.A. in experimental psychology in 1981 and is pursuing her doctoral degree. Judith Sugar obtained her Ph.D. in developmental psychology in 1981 at York University and is currently doing post-doctoral work. All three authors are at the University of Cincinnati.